THE LEAFS

THE LEAFS

BRIAN
McFARLANE'S
ORIGINAL
SIX

BRIAN McFARLANE

Published in 1995 by
Stoddart Publishing Co. Limited
34 Lesmill Road
Toronto, Canada M3B 2T6
Tel. (416) 445-3333
Fax (416) 445-5967

Stoddart Books are available for bulk purchase for sales
promotions, premiums, fundraising, and seminars. For details,
contact the **Special Sales Department** at the above address.

Canadian Cataloguing in Publication Data

McFarlane, Brian, 1931–
The Leafs

(Brian McFarlane's original six)
ISBN 0-7737-2913-5

1. Toronto Maple Leafs (Hockey team) – History.
I. Title. II. Series: McFarlane, Brian, 1931–
Brian McFarlane's original six

GV848.T6M34   1995   796.962'64'09713541
C95-931223-4

Cover design: Bill Douglas at The Bang
Text design: Kinetics Design & Illustration

Printed and bound in Canada

Stoddart Publishing gratefully acknowledges
the support of the Canada Council, the Ontario Ministry of
Citizenship, Culture and Recreation, Ontario Arts Council, and
Ontario Publishing Centre in the development of writing and
publishing in Canada.

Contents

3
The Forties

The Fifties

The Sixties

6

The Seventies

7

The Eighties and Nineties

Introduction

HE'S an old lady now, surviving on borrowed time. Soon Maple Leaf Gardens, like the Montreal Forum, the Boston Garden, and the Chicago Stadium, will be forsaken and ignored. A new home for the Leafs will spring up, costing at least $100 million more than the old maid on Carlton Street when she debuted in 1931. Years will pass and old geezers like me will bore our grandchildren with tales that begin, "Did I ever tell you about a place called Maple Leaf Gardens, where the Leafs used to play, and the first hockey game I ever saw there back in '38?"

I'll tell them about being a wide-eyed kid, no bigger than a goal pad, and how I clutched my dad's arm as we waded through the crowd on Carlton Street, were swept through the lobby, and funnelled through the clicking turnstiles and on into the mammoth arena. It was incredibly huge, full of lights and seats and glistening ice. Soon it was filled with thousands of excited fans, all of them there to witness Billy Taylor and the Oshawa Generals clash with Wally Stanowski and the invaders from St. Boniface. I had no idea where St. Boniface was but I knew all about Billy Taylor. My dad had written a story about him and sold it to *Maclean's* or *Liberty* — I've forgotten which.

Taylor and Stanowski are the only players I remember from that game. Their speed and playmaking ability triggered howls of delight and groans of despair from the fans around me, many of whom leaped to their feet and spoiled my view whenever the goalies were threatened. When we got home my dad told my mother about my fascination for hockey and how I never took my eyes off the action — until he mentioned an ice-cream bar or a hot dog. Then he almost went broke keeping me supplied.

There was a second game, this one an NHL game between the Leafs and the New York Rangers. It was just as big a thrill to be at the Gardens a second time. Mr. Dent took me to this game. He was sweet on one of the two schoolteachers who boarded at our house in Whitby, and they may have married but I don't know for sure. I'll always be grateful to Mr. Dent for taking me to my first Leaf game. I saw Syl Apps perform that night and he became my hockey idol. The Leaf captain came to Whitby once and my dad walked me down the street and into this smoke-filled hall where a group of cigar-smoking men were grouped around the hockey star. We squeezed our way into the centre of the pack and my dad told Syl I'd like an autograph.

I held my scrap of paper up and Mr. Apps leaned over to sign it. I'm sure I didn't say a word but I remember his broad smile and how strong and fit he looked. He was more handsome than all the other men in the room. But then, hockey heroes always look sensational to their young fans, don't you think? Just above his signature I noticed he'd added two extra words: Best wishes, Syl Apps. That was a nice surprise. I carried that scrap of paper to school the next day and showed it to everybody. Like most autographs, it disappeared in time. I wish I had it today. That signature meant a lot to me.

Years later, in the '60s, on occasion I would sit next to Syl Apps in the press box at the Gardens. It was then located at the south end of the building, next to the organ loft. Even then, as an adult and an experienced broadcaster, I felt privileged to be conversing with the famous Leaf legend, for childhood idols are never forgotten. He chuckled when I told him how proud I was to get his autograph that night in Whitby.

In time I would meet Billy Taylor as well, and Wally Stanowski. Taylor, barred from hockey for life in 1948 for associating with gamblers, had been reinstated by then and was an NHL scout. Stanowski would become a teammate on the NHL Oldtimers, a club I was invited to join one night as an amateur fill-in for a game. I stayed with them for the next 17 seasons.

Some of our Oldtimer games were played at the Gardens before thousands of fans. As the only non-NHLer on the ice, I was thrilled to be out there. With the Oldtimers I always felt I represented the thousands of players who, like me, played decent hockey, but lacked the abundant skills the NHLers possessed. We were the ones who never made it. But there I was at the Gardens one night, playing against Ted Lindsay, Gordie Howe, and Leo Reise of the Red Wing Oldtimers. On my first shift Red Storey, the referee, thumbed me off with a penalty. "One minute for impersonating Foster Hewitt," he announced to the crowd.

Behind our bench were two of the greatest coaches, Joe Primeau and Punch Imlach. And King Clancy was there too — all three Hall-of-Famers and Stanley Cup winners. Imagine me being coached by *them!*

But I digress. Growing up, I suppose it never occurred to me that every young hockey fan, on his or her first visit to Maple Leaf Gardens, was just as goose-bumpy with excitement as I was. I wrote a column for the Gardens hockey program a few years ago and a man named James Emmerson, rewrite chief at the old Toronto *Telegram*, was kind enough to send me his impressions of *his* first Gardens visit. James began by revealing a surprising fact: Leaf stars used to come out and referee the games he played in as a kid. Here's how James remembered it:

Modesty has kept me silent for years. Now I'm going to brag a bit. Once, I shared the ice lanes with some of hockey's greatest — Primeau, Jackson, Conacher, Hainsworth and Horner. And not one of them could lay a stick on me! You see, they were referees in our Midget National Hockey League and they weren't allowed to.

The Midget NHL — now known as the Little NHL — was founded decades ago by Gordon Alcott of George-town, Ontario. Ninety boys were in that first group, now there are thousands. In the Depression-day '30s we stuffed our stockings with catalogues and our stomachs with Bee Hive Corn Syrup, assured by radio broadcaster Wes McKnight that the latter would help produce a board-bending shot like Charlie Conacher's.

We scavenged broken sticks from Intermediate teams and nailed, wired and taped them together. After school, we batted tin cans up and down the road. And all the while we dreamed.

We dreamed of becoming big league hockey stars, of scoring the winning goal in the final seconds to give the Leafs the Stanley Cup. In this boyhood fantasy, the Prime Minister himself would shuffle warily onto the ice to congratulate us.

Gordon Alcott brought a bit of that dream true for us when he convinced Conn Smythe to send out some Leaf stars to referee our games. But Major Smythe went a step further. He offered the use of Maple Leaf Gardens for the Midget NHL on very special occasions.

Gord sent us into the streets of Georgetown to sell "booster tickets" to help finance sweaters and stockings. Several firms and business groups gave each of the six teams $25.00. Could even one boy be outfitted for that today? Eventually we took to the ice in sweaters emblazoned with the names of our hockey heroes of the day — Shore, Morenz, Schriner and Seibert — the Hull, Howe, Orr and Mikita of their time.

King Clancy refereed our first game. The league was an instant success. But I wasn't. My scoring record that first year read: Goals, none; Assists, none; Shots on goal, none: Shots on goalkeeper — ONE! With a wild clearing shot I had hit the shins of the referee — the great netminder Lorne Chabot.

But the biggest adventure that season was being taken to see a game at Maple Leaf Gardens. We went in the back of Dick Licata's fruit truck. Soggy cabbage leaves and crushed banana stocks were swept out. Orange crates and butter boxes were installed for seats. A tarpaulin overhead sealed out light and wind but not the cold.

Do you know who rode with us that day? Under the tarp with the rest of us was Bob Goldham, who would grow up to star on defense for the Leafs. As the Little NHL spread across the province it spawned other great NHL stars like Bob Pulford, George Armstrong and Tim Horton. But Bob Goldham was the only one of the original ninety to make it big. Gordie Howe not long ago gave Bob something better than a trophy ten feet tall when he picked him on his all-time all-star Detroit team.

But all of this glory for one of our number was far in the unknown future that day. We jostled up to the Gardens on our butter boxes beneath that dark, damp, cold tarpaulin.

Oh, I know some of you will tell me there's no thrill in the world like a visit to the Taj Mahal or to Disneyland. Take them all, I say. You can have them. For I have had the thrill that will last me a lifetime.

I walked with that gangly group of bug-eyed kids, blinking our way from the gloom in the back of Dick Licata's fruit truck into that incredible canyon of color, humanity, noise and excitement that was — and still is — Maple Leaf Gardens.

It was in the vast edifice on Carlton Street where some of the greatest hockey games and most memorable series were played out back in the days of the original six NHL clubs. Imagine Toronto playing Montreal 14 times a season, seven games at home and seven away. One Saturday night the Gardens would be invaded by the Flying Frenchmen — the Richards, Beliveau, and Plante. You'd catch your breath from that game in time to greet Detroit with big Howe, Delvecchio, and Sawchuk. A week later, Bobby Hull, Stan Mikita, and durable Glenn Hall, who never missed a game, would create all the excitement. It was a fabulous time to be involved with hockey, as a fan, a player, a broadcaster.

In this initial volume, I'll focus on Toronto players and teams in the era of the original six, with five more volumes to follow involving original sixers Montreal, Boston, New York, Detroit, and Chicago. Allow me the freedom to set the stage with a look beyond the era, to a time when there were no Toronto Maple Leafs. And let me follow some original-six players into the woeful Ballard Years, as they wound down their colourful careers long after six teams became 12, then 14, then 26, to whatever number the NHL may have embraced by the time this reaches print.

If you're a Leaf fan or just a hockey fan, why not come on along for the ride? We'll try to make it interesting, we'll try to make it fun.

Brian McFarlane

1

BEFORE THE
BUILDING OF THE
GARDENS

Toronto's First Cup Champs

THE inaugural season of the NHL was an agonizing one and when a Toronto team — the Arenas — skated off with the Stanley Cup in the spring of 1918, league organizers must have been concerned about the future of hockey in Canada. For the newly-formed league's initial season had produced a series of threats, headaches, squabbles, and bewildering events.

On the eve of the NHL opener in Montreal, the owner of the Montreal Arena said he was fed up with the poor calibre of hockey displayed by the two NHL clubs based there — Canadiens and Wanderers — and threatened to turf them both out of his rink and reserve the ice for pleasure skating if the locals didn't shape up.

The Wanderers won their first game over Toronto 10–9. It was wartime and soldiers in uniform were invited to fill the empty seats for the home opener. Little did the Wanderers know that their first victory would also be their last. A few days later the Montreal Arena burned to the ground, forcing the Wanderers (with a 1–3 record and 35 goals against) to withdraw from the circuit. Earlier, the Quebec franchise had disbanded, leaving only three teams — Canadiens, Ottawa, and Toronto — to compete.

When Ottawa skated out for a game in Toronto in January, the visitors' bench was empty. There were no substitutes. Toronto obliged by emptying their bench. It was the only NHL game ever played with a minimum of 12 players involved.

Later that month, Bad Joe Hall of Montreal and Alf Skinner of Toronto tried to decapitate each other in a vicious stick-swinging duel. Both were arrested and hauled into court, where a lenient judge released them with suspended sentences.

Two Toronto stars, Harry Cameron and Reg Noble, were fined $100 each by management after they refused to play in a game at Montreal in February. They had also been caught breaking training.

Toronto tough guy Ken Randall was fined $15 by the league for lambasting the game officials. He was suspended until he paid the fine, plus back fines of $20. Randall grudgingly coughed up $32 in bills and some rolled coins totalling three dollars. These he tossed on the ice, where a player whacked the roll with his stick, spilling pennies in all directions.

The Jubilee Rink in Montreal was so tiny that one Montreal game was transferred to Quebec City, where scoring whiz Joe Malone had played the year before. Malone, picked up by Montreal when the Quebec team disbanded, scored 44 goals in 20 games in the NHL's first season, establishing a record that remains unmatched.

Toronto and Montreal met in the two-game, total-goals-to-count NHL finals and Toronto won out 10–7. Both games were described as slugfests.

Toronto went on to capture the Stanley Cup over Vancouver, the PCHA champions, winning three games to two on home ice. The westerners wore very little padding and were pounded by the more aggressive Arenas. The fifth game was tied 1–1 in the third period when Toronto's Corb Denneny, who had tallied 20 goals in 21 league games, broke through to slam in the winning goal and become Toronto's first NHL playoff hero.

It was a Corb Denneny goal that propelled another Toronto team — St. Patricks — into the Stanley Cup finals again in 1922. After another 20-goal season, Denneny scored the winning goal against Ottawa in the 1922 NHL playoffs. His marker advanced St. Pats into the Stanley Cup finals against Vancouver. Toronto sharpshooter Babe Dye, with 11 goals in seven games, was the playoff hero as Toronto captured the Stanley Cup for the second time under the banner of the NHL. Note: In 1914, prior to the formation of the NHL, the National Hockey Association (NHA) Toronto Blue Shirts, playing before small crowds, defeated Victoria, B.C., to bring Toronto its first Stanley Cup.

It would be another 10 years before Toronto would claim a fourth Stanley Cup. By then the city's hockey powerhouse would be known as Maple Leafs. They would be performing in a world-class arena before sellout crowds and guided by the firm hand of a controversial, colourful hockey visionary: Constantine Falkland Kerrys (Conn) Smythe.

How the Leafs Got Their Name

WHO invented the name "Maple Leafs"? It certainly wasn't team owner Conn Smythe, although many credit him for the appealing appellation. There were at least two clubs named Leafs long before Smythe came along and both were Stanley Cup challengers. Smythe may have borrowed the moniker from a defunct hockey team — the 1908 Toronto Maple Leafs of the Ontario Professional League. That circuit, the first outright professional loop, was better known as the Trolley League because teams were bunched together within an hour or two of Toronto and travelled to games by the trolley lines that connected the centres.

In 1908, the Toronto Maple Leafs captured the Trolley League championship. Led by superstar Newsy Lalonde, who had scored 29 goals in just nine league games, the early-day Leafs challenged the mighty Montreal Wanderers for the Stanley Cup. By a strange coincidence a Winnipeg team, also bearing the name Maple Leafs, were Cup challengers too — and first in line to battle the Wanderers for the Cup that same season.

In a two-game series the Wanderers crushed the Manitoba Leafs by scores of 11–5 and 9–3 and then met the Toronto Leafs in a single game with the Stanley Cup at stake. Nobody gave the Toronto invaders a chance. Hadn't the Wanderers, during the 1907 season, averaged over 10 goals a game? Hadn't their star player, Ernie Russell, potted 42 goals in the nine games he played — over four per game!

Wanderer fans confidently predicted another lopsided triumph and wagered huge sums that their heroes would double the score on Toronto. Imagine their chagrin when they lost their shirts on the match. Oh, the Wanderers won the game, and slipped away with Lord Stanley's precious mug at the end of the day. But the score was tied four times and the Stanley Cup champs had to produce some late-game heroics to win by the narrowest of margins, 6–4.

With the Leafs trailing 4–3, Toronto's Newsy Lalonde scored one of the strangest goals in playoff history. During a lull in the action, the Wanderers, including goalie Riley Hern, were beckoned to the sideboards by their fans. Montreal supporters were almost in tears at the thought of losing all the money they'd so willingly wagered with the smug interlopers from Ontario. They urged the Wanderers to fill the Toronto net with pucks. Handsome bonuses were promised if only they'd double the score.

While this animated meeting was going on between Wanderers and wagerers, the referee grew impatient. He dropped the puck at centre ice and Newsy Lalonde snapped it up. With no opposing players between him and the open net, he snapped a shot half the length of the rink — and scored! That triggered a furious argument from the Wanderers, but the referee turned a deaf ear and Lalonde's empty-netter tied the score at four. The angry Wanderers stormed back to win the contest 6–4 and retain the Cup. The result appeared to pacify the Montreal fans, although most of the wagerers went home with empty pockets.

Conn Smythe may have remembered that gritty performance by Newsy Lalonde and his Maple Leaf mates. Then again, perhaps he considered adopting the Maple Leaf name for his team as a tribute to the Toronto Granites' incredible performance at the 1924 Olympics in Chamonix, France. The players on the Granites, men like Hooley Smith, Dunc Munro, and Beattie Ramsay — all three future stars in the NHL — wore maple leaf crests on their jerseys during play on the open-air rink in Chamonix. The Granites stunned their rivals in the eight-country tournament, outscoring the opposition 110–3 in the five games played. Toronto's Harry Watson scored 38 goals alone. The Canadian goalie, emulating Riley Hern perhaps, left his post once or twice in the tournament and skated over to the sideboards, not to talk wagering but to chat with two lovely mademoiselles about hockey and other matters.

For whatever reasons, Smythe liked the name Maple Leafs and adopted it. He himself had worn the symbol proudly on badges and on uniform patches while serving his country during the war.

He wanted a name that reflected his fervor for his nation, a name that would last for decades. Previous pro teams in Toronto had skated as Blue Shirts, Arenas, and St. Pats. Smythe was not impressed. He wanted nothing to do with those bland names, especially St. Patricks, which a previous manager had concocted in hopes of attracting the Irish in Toronto to pro games.

When Smythe offered to purchase the St. Patricks franchise in January of 1927, with $10,000 down and the promise of another $75,000 two weeks later, the deal was all but complete. Smythe was able to raise the money and the faltering franchise was his. He promptly declared that the team colours would be changed from green and white to blue and white and henceforth the team would be known as the Maple Leafs. Who could have known then what a fascinating future lay ahead for Smythe and the men associated with his bold purchase?

The Great Inter-City Feud

DURING the 1916–17 NHA season, in the midst of World War I, a furious battle raged in Toronto between the Blue Shirts and an upstart army team, the 228th Battalion. It was a torrid rivalry that ended only when the army players traded in their sticks for rifles and went overseas to do battle with Germany. By the time they returned, the 228th Battalion was just a sliver of hockey history and a new league — the NHL — was experiencing birth pains.

Few people remember the 228th, the first, last, and only military unit to be involved in professional hockey. It was an era when volunteers for military service were praised and applauded, but not so the hockey-playing members of the 228th. They were loathed by the Blue Shirts and their many supporters.

It began when the great Duke Keats, along with Archie Briden, a lesser star, bolted from the Blue Shirts to join the army. They were promptly assigned to the 228th and joined such luminaries as the McNamara brothers, Goldie Prodgers, Butch Arbour, Art Duncan, and others. The boys in khaki promptly whipped an NHA All-Star team 10–0.

The owner of the Blue Shirts, Eddie Livingstone, screamed like a banshee over the loss of Keats and Briden. "They're my players," he insisted. "They signed contracts to play for me. Now the army has them and I want them back. They can still serve their country but when they play, they play for me."

After some bitter wrangling, war or no war, Keats and Briden left the 228th and suited up for the Blues. Peace between the two clubs, apparently restored, lasted only a few days. Early in 1917 they tangled for the first time and the soldiers won 4–0 in a penalty-filled game. Three weeks later the 228th won again, beating the Blues 8–6. In this game there was a trail of cracked skulls as players on both sides indulged in butt ends, flying elbows, and swinging sticks. Keats showed his versatility in this match by taking over in goal when the Blues' netminder was sent off to the penalty box. Keats was not scored on. The third and final meeting took place on February 7. Prior to the game there were rumours that Keats and Briden had broken some army rules and were in the guardhouse, and therefore were unavailable to play for the Blues. The uproar created by Livingstone may have had something to do with their release because both players were liberated in time for the big game. The Blues won the match 4–3 with players belting each other all over the ice.

A few days after the game, some army officers huddled and announced that they were disgusted with professional hockey and were suspending hockey operations of the 228th. "If the soldiers are going to be maimed, it might as well be in France and not on Canadian ice," said one. So the 228th went off to Europe where they played "for keeps." Their departure marked the end of the Great Toronto Hockey Feud, a short-lived but bitter hockey rivalry.

Eddie Livingstone's Frustration

EDDIE Livingstone was the fiery and quarrelsome owner of the Toronto Blue Shirts in 1916, and he was furious when the NHA directors, at a meeting in Montreal, suspended his club for the balance of the 1916–17 season. Livingstone's team was thrown out for "transgressions of the rules," although the league moguls were slow to set out which rules had been transgressed. Several of Livingstone's players were assigned to other clubs in the (now) four-team league, with the understanding that those players would return to the Blue Shirts at season's end.

The directors must have chuckled among themselves when they contemplated the fate of Mr. Livingstone. For they had decided, you may be sure, that his litany of complaints, raised by his argumentative voice, would no longer be heard during league meetings. Within months, all of the existing clubs resigned from the NHA and promptly formed the foundation of a new league — the National Hockey League. Livingstone was left stranded in Toronto with a good team but no league to play in.

Boiling over in anger and frustration, Livingstone fought back. In a bizarre move, he and his cronies, in a military-type operation, seized the Jubilee Rink in Montreal. He left a handful of his recruits there with orders to hold the fort. They didn't hold it long. When George Kennedy, an ex-wrestler and owner of the Montreal Canadiens, heard about the coup, he assembled a number of his burly wrestling pals and marched on the arena. The Livingstone forces were quickly routed. Livingstone later launched a lawsuit against his former colleagues, but he lost the case and soon disappeared from the hockey scene.

Toronto Team Scores 20 Goals in First Two NHL Tilts

WHEN the NHL made its debut in 1917, the Toronto entry known as the Arenas scored more goals in its first two games than any other Queen City club past or present. The Arenas hit for 20 goals — 9 in the opener at Montreal against the Wanderers and 11 two nights later on home ice versus Ottawa. Despite the scoring binge the Toronto club lost the first game 10–9. In the opener at Montreal all soldiers were invited to attend the game as guests of Wanderer president Sam Lichtenhein, but only a few took advantage of the offer. The attendance numbered 700, including those attired in khaki.

Ottawa was no match for Toronto in game two, losing 11–4. If it hadn't been for the solid work of Clint Benedict in the Ottawa goal, the home team might easily have scored half a dozen more times.

In the first four NHL games ever played, the scorers dominated, collecting a total of 58 goals.

Getting Rid of Herberts

PRIOR to the 1927–28 NHL season, Conn Smythe let himself be sweet-talked by Boston's Art Ross, who was to become an archenemy. Perhaps the antagonism began with the purchase of Jimmy (Sailor) Herberts.

Smythe took a chance and bought Herberts from the Bruins for $12,500. Herberts arrived in due time and introduced his wife to the Leaf owner. Smythe recalls that her skirts were "extremely short, and they seemed to get shorter every time she moved around in her chair." Herberts and his bride made it clear that they were not happy with the deal that brought him to Toronto. His wife in particular was quite vocal in her complaints about the city.

Smythe soon discovered that Herberts's skills on the ice had eroded. Ross, he concluded, had stuck him with a has-been, a big lemon of a player. The night Herberts stepped on the Gardens' ice for the first time, not only did he fall on his face coming through the gate but he lined up with the opposing team. The fans roasted him with their boos.

Smythe had seen enough. He called Detroit and told manager Charlie Hughes that the Herbertses, player and wife, were very unhappy in Toronto. But they loved Detroit. Herberts's wife, he added, was from Windsor and Smythe was certain Herberts would regain his old form if he could play for Detroit.

Hughes, somewhat skeptical, said he'd watch Herberts closely the next time the Leafs were in town.

On that occasion, Smythe huddled with his players. He told them he must get rid of Herberts and at a good price. Otherwise he might go broke and there'd be no wages for the rest of them. He urged them to "make Herberts look good against Detroit."

His players got the message. They fed Herberts dozens of passes that night and he clicked for goals on two or three of them. He played like an All-Star. The Detroit manager was impressed and quickly met Smythe's demand of $15,000 for Herberts.

Herberts actually played reasonably well for Detroit and scored nine goals that season. But after scoring just one goal the following year, he bowed out of big-league hockey.

By then, Smythe had spent most of the $15,000 on acquiring players he liked much better.

Caught at the Border

DURING the days of Prohibition in the United States, it was customary for Canadians visiting the United States to bring along a bottle or two of an American friend's favourite beverage, one of those potent elixirs that was quite legal to imbibe in Canada but, alas, banned below the border.

Prior to a long train ride with his Leafs to New York in 1928, Conn Smythe and his portly trainer, Tim Daly, each purchased two bottles of grog which they planned to deliver to thirsty pals living in Manhattan. By sheer coincidence, they had purchased the same brand of liquor.

Before arriving at U.S. Customs in Fort Erie, Smythe tossed his two bottles to Daly and ordered him to "stow this booze out of sight until we cross the border." Smythe was aware that the penalty for importing or transporting booze over the border could be as much as five years in jail and a $10,000 fine.

Daly dutifully obeyed but the customs officials were only half fooled. When the train chugged away, Daly scurried to Smythe's compartment, clutching two bottles to his chest.

"Boss," he stammered. "Guess what? Those customs guys grabbed the two crocks you bought. But they decided not to press charges against you."

Smythe calmly plucked a bottle out of Daly's grasp, held it aloft, and eyed it under the light.

"No, Tim, this appears to be one of mine," he laughed. "And the other one must be yours. That means they got one from both of us."

Daly was left speechless — a rarity for him.

Oldtimers say he had a gift for language, a gift for mangling it like few others in hockey. During the '50s, at the height of the Korean War, he exhorted the Leafs in the dressing room one night. "Boys, let's win this one tonight for all those brave young lads fighting over there in Kenora!"

Sid Smith recalls the time Daly slipped away to see an afternoon movie. Smith asked him, "What movie did you see, Tim?"

"A good one, Smitty. It was called *Un-concurred.*"

Smith was puzzled. Then he recalled that there was a John Wayne epic playing in town.

"Tim, you mean *Unconquered?*"

"Yeah, sumpin like that."

Jockey Claims Credit for Clancy Trade

NORMAN "The Dude" Foden, a jockey until he was 55, often claimed credit for the deal that brought King Clancy to Toronto. He even went a step further and bragged that he was largely responsible for the building of Maple Leaf Gardens.

Foden's link to the Clancy trade began on September 30, 1930, with the running of the Coronation Stakes. Smythe owned a filly named Rare Jewel, a horse he purchased for a mere $250, a nag that had lost every race she'd entered. When Smythe decided to enter Rare Jewel in the big race, his trainer said, "Why bother? The horse can't win."

"Dude" Foden disagreed. "She has a chance, Mr. Smythe," he said. "Let's give it a shot." Smythe noted Rare Jewel's number on the program — number 7 — and her post position — number 11. "Seven come eleven," he chuckled. "Sounds pretty good to a superstitious guy like me. I'm going to bet a bundle." So Smythe placed his bets. Ironically, when Foden's wife asked his advice on the race, he told her, "Bet Froth Blower, the favourite."

Years later, Foden could still remember the details of the race:

Four days earlier, I had ridden Rare Jewel in the mud at Montreal and she finished 18 lengths behind the winner.

Imagine being beaten 18 lengths and winning the Coronation at Woodbine just four days later.

There's a story that goes with it, of course. I told Mr. Smythe not to bet the filly at Montreal. You see, Dave Garrity, a pal of mine, had a horse named Ethel Kenyon in the race. I was leading going into the first turn and I took the entire field to the outside, I mean almost out to the fence. All but Ethel Kenyon, that is. She slipped in along the rail and won easy. Remember, I said Dave Garrity was a good friend of mine.

Now we come to the Coronation and Rare Jewel had shown me something in her final workout. So Mr. Smythe paid the $40 starting fee and he bet fifty bucks on her across the board. What a ribbing he took from his pals who were there. So Conn got mad and bet another thirty bucks on her to win.

Well sir, in the race, there was some rough riding before I slipped Rare Jewel in on the rail as we turned for home and caught the jockey on Froth Blower by surprise. Rare Jewel forged into the lead by a couple of lengths and here comes Froth Blower in hot pursuit. But I kept my horse in front all the way to the wire with Froth Blower closing fast and finishing a half length back. They fined me later for rough riding, and I served a three-day suspension. But it was worth it. Sure it was worth it. I always figured Mr. Smythe would never have finished building Maple Leaf Gardens if I hadn't won that Coronation.

Rare Jewel went off at odds of 107–1 and paid $214.40 for a two dollar wager. Never won another race. Smythe cashed tickets for over $12,000 and added the winner's purse of $3,570 to his total. What a payoff!

Smythe went straight to the directors of the Toronto Maple Leafs and said, "Gentlemen, you told me I could spend up to $25,000 to purchase King Clancy from Ottawa. It's going to take a lot more than that to get him. I'll throw in my race track winnings and a couple of fringe players and we'll engineer the biggest trade in hockey history."

Clancy's team, the Ottawa Senators, needed money badly. Ottawa asked for $35,000 and players Art Smith and Eric Pettinger. Smythe agreed to the terms and Clancy became a Leaf.

The Toronto *Globe* assessed Clancy as "one of the three most colourful players in the world, along with Howie Morenz and Eddie Shore."

In the months that followed, whenever he saw Clancy play or heard him talked about, "Dude" Foden, the diminutive jockey, never failed to say, "I'm the guy who helped get him to Toronto — me and Rare Jewel. Conn Smythe might have finished building the Gardens without us but he might not have filled it night after night without Clancy. And we brought him Clancy."

And when the Leafs won the Stanley Cup in 1932, the first season of play in the Gardens, no doubt Foden shook his small head in disbelief when the engraver failed to etch his name on the Cup.

"He coulda put it there," Foden grinned. "Me and Rare Jewel — right there next to Clancy's name." He winked. "Don't you think we deserve it?"

Clancy's Cunning
Saves the Leafs from a Loss

ON March 10, 1931, the Leafs and the Bruins skated to a 3–3 tie at the Boston Garden in a game that netted the Bruins first place in the American Division of the NHL.

But it was in the fiercely-played overtime period that Leaf stalwart King Clancy concocted an idea that saved the Leafs from instant defeat. Toronto goalie Lorne Chabot stopped a difficult shot with his chest and in trying to clear the puck lost it within his equipment. Referee Mickey Ion rushed in and ordered a face-off in front of Chabot, claiming that the goalie had deliberately held the puck. Seconds later, Bruin star Cooney Weiland won the draw from Joe Primeau and slapped the puck past Chabot for the winning goal.

But wait! King Clancy rushed up to linesman Bill Shaver and stated that he was offside when the puck was faced off. He claimed that Ion was so anxious to drop the puck that he hadn't given Clancy enough time to get into proper position. Why Shaver even listened to King is anybody's guess. The fans were whooping it up, the Bruins were congratulating one another, and most of the Leafs were already skating off the ice. For Shaver, a Boston native, to side with Clancy could only lead to a lot of aggravation.

But Shaver didn't hesitate. He called Ion over and said, "Mickey, I have to agree with King. I think he was offside on the play. You'd better disallow the goal and face the puck off again."

"Christ, Bill," snorted Ion. "You know these Bruin fans. They think they've just salted away first place. They'll throw everything at us if we take the goal away."

"I'm just telling you what I think," said Shaver.

Bracing himself for the abuse that followed, Ion disallowed the goal by Weiland. The crowd howled its displeasure, Ion ducked a ton of debris hurled in his direction, and the Boston players angrily questioned his morals, his ancestry, and his intelligence.

Clancy, smirking off to the side, said to a teammate, "For once, I talked the officials into changing their minds."

When the ice was cleared, another faceoff was held in front of Chabot. This time, Primeau snared the puck and cleared it down the ice. Chabot, given another chance to shine, held off the Bruins until time ran out and the game was declared a 3–3 tie.

Ion was happy to put the game behind him. Earlier in the contest, he'd triggered another confrontation when he ordered Conn Smythe and Frank Selke to leave the Toronto players' bench. But they refused to budge and a long argument had developed, with Boston owner Weston Adams joining in for no good reason. Ion won that battle, only to face Clancy's challenge in the overtime frame.

"Those Leafs are always finding new ways to give me a headache," Ion complained to Shaver.

Smythe, Primeau Rejected by Rangers

WHEN Conn Smythe was hired by the New York Rangers in 1926 and given the task of finding players for the new NHL franchise, the first man he signed was a lightweight centreman from Toronto named Joe Primeau.

But Smythe was soon replaced by Lester Patrick. They wanted "a more experienced hockey man," the New York owners said when asked to explain the change.

There are two versions of the story behind Primeau's return to Toronto. One is that Patrick looked at the pasty-faced Primeau, wondered why Smythe would have bothered with him, and sold him to Toronto for $500. The other is that Smythe was smart enough to sign Primeau to a personal services contract and when he left, Joe left with him.

It wasn't long before both Smythe and Primeau gained sweet revenge for the shabby treatment they'd received from the Rangers. In 1932, the Leafs, led by Smythe the owner and Primeau the slick centreman on the famous Kid Line, captured the Stanley Cup, winning three straight games from Patrick's Rangers.

Joe Primeau was an outstanding player who turned to coaching after he retired from the Leafs in 1936. He coached teams that won the Memorial Cup, the Allan Cup, and the Stanley Cup, which he captured in his first season as Leaf coach in 1951. He was inducted into the Hockey Hall of Fame in 1963.

Babe's Mother Taught Him Well

CECIL "Babe" Dye was just a little guy but when it came to shooting a puck he was right up there with Conacher. And it was his mother who taught him how.

Early in the century, it was Essie Dye who flooded the backyard rink, laced up Babe's skates, and supervised his skating and shooting drills. Babe's father had passed away shortly after his son's birth and Essie, a natural athlete herself, was determined that Babe would make a name for himself in athletics.

The backyard drills paid off. Soon Babe could shoot the puck from any spot on the rink and whip it at a makeshift goal with amazing accuracy. He excelled at all sports and might easily have become a major league ballplayer if his first love hadn't been hockey.

At age 18, during one season, he scored 12 goals against rival goalies without having to cross centre ice. When fans and reporters expressed amazement at this feat, he laughed and said, "Aw, my mom could have scored those goals standing back on our goal line. And she can throw a baseball harder than I can."

Dye played for Toronto St. Pats for seven seasons and in the Stanley Cup finals of 1922, playing against Vancouver, he scored a famous "invisible" goal, a marker discussed by fans for years afterwards. There was a faceoff at the Vancouver blue line and the puck came back to Dye. He flicked his wrists and shot with such blinding speed that Hughie Lehman, the Vancouver goalie, crouching in his crease, didn't move a muscle. Some of the players and the game officials skated around in confusion. Nobody on the ice seemed to know what had happened. But the fans in back of the Vancouver goal knew. And Babe Dye knew. Smiling, he skated back to line up for the ensuing faceoff at centre ice. Finally goalie Lehman and the officials spotted the puck nestled in the twine in the Vancouver goal. They couldn't believe it had arrived there, almost unseen.

Dye tied for the scoring lead in the NHL that season with 30 goals in 24 games. Then he topped all playoff scorers with 11 goals in seven games and led Toronto to the Stanley Cup.

For the first seven years of his NHL career, he averaged over a goal a game: 174 goals in 170 games. Traded to Chicago prior to the 1927 season, he enjoyed a 25-goal season before suffering a broken leg. The injury affected his skating and caused his goal production to plummet. He scored just one goal in his final three seasons.

Smythe Dismissed for Failing to Sign Dye

IF Toronto St. Pats star Babe Dye had a weakness it was his penchant for individual play. His goal-scoring ability placed him in the spotlight and he enjoyed the glare. If his teammates were often overlooked, too bad. As a result, Babe was not the most popular player with those who skated with him.

Conn Smythe knew Babe for what he was and Smythe wanted only team players on the clubs he managed. When Smythe was hired to put together the New York Rangers in 1926, Dye was available. Smythe said "no thanks" when asked if he'd take him. New York owner Colonel Hammond was furious with his young manager. He didn't know much about hockey but he knew that Dye had a reputation for scoring goals — lots of goals. He practically ordered Smythe to get Dye's signature on a Ranger contract. Smythe's retort: "Colonel, I don't want Babe Dye on my team."

With that, Hammond began muttering to cronies that perhaps Smythe wasn't the man for the Ranger job after all. Several of his flunkies agreed with him. Before long Hammond began wooing veteran hockey manager Lester Patrick and prior to the first game of the new season, Smythe was dismissed and replaced by Patrick. Two years later the team Smythe had assembled in New York won the Stanley Cup. By then Babe Dye wasn't scoring any goals at all and his career was virtually over.

No Puck, No Game

THE 1925–26 season turned out to be one of frustration for the Toronto St. Pats, soon to become the Toronto Maple Leafs. The team won only 12 games and lost 21. One of those losses was by forfeit.

On the night of February 27, the St. Pats and the Canadiens mixed it up in a brawl, one that included players from both clubs, the fans, and the police. With order restored the referee looked for the puck and found it in the glove of Leaf captain Cecil "Babe" Dye.

"Gimme the puck!" said Bobby Hewitson, the diminutive official.

"I will not," answered the angry captain.

For whatever reason, Dye refused to give up the rubber and Hewitson didn't bother to seek out another. He simply skated off the ice and awarded the game to Montreal.

2

BEFORE THE ORIGINAL SIX

First Night

O N the night of November 12, 1931, Maple Leaf Gardens was overflowing with pomp and circumstance. It was opening night and somewhere, somehow, over 13,500 eager fans had scraped together the price of admission ($1.80 for a good seat in the blues), blown another 15 cents for a program, and listened to a parade of windy politicians praise the edifice and its principal owner, Mr. Conn Smythe. While they droned on, fans kept screaming, "Play hockey! Play hockey!"

Charlie Good, then a young usher, earned 50 cents that evening escorting people, many of them in evening attire, to their seats. "The building was still full of junk and construction supplies," Charlie recalled years later. "But it was all pushed aside for the opening game with Chicago."

The Blackhawks' Harold (Mush) March scored the first-ever goal at the Gardens. Charlie Conacher tied the score with the first Toronto goal. But Chicago's Vic Ripley scored the game-winner in a 2–1 victory for the visitors.

Half a century passed. By then Charlie Good was earning $3.75 an hour and was still ushering people to their seats. Long-time Gardens ushers like Good could remember fans fainting in their seats, or suffering heart attacks from the excitement of the games. Spectators were often struck with flying pucks and led off to the medical room for treatment. Sometimes fans fought with other fans. There were always surprises, both on and off the ice. At least once during a Leaf game a woman had a miscarriage. Good remembered a fan who was so drunk he slept through three periods of play, then was nudged awake by an usher who was asked, "When's the game start, bud?" A bare-ass fan, showing every little thing, streaked naked across the Gardens' ice surface one night in the middle of our *Hockey Night in Canada* telecast.

For years, fans in rinkside seats dressed to the hilt for hockey games. Shirts, jackets, and ties were compulsory for the males. Owner Conn Smythe demanded proper attire and held the threat of cancelled season tickets over the heads of his customers in case they showed up in shoddy clothes.

Even the biggest of the brass were reprimanded for bending the rules. When Evelyn O'Ryan of North York worked as an usherette at the Gardens in the '70s, she ordered Leaf owner Harold Ballard to put out his cigar and later ordered Johnny Bassett, owner of the Toronto Toros, to do the same thing.

The First Great Goalie

MOST hockey fans are familiar with the famous story of Lester Patrick, and how, at age 44, he led the New York Rangers as coach — and as substitute goalie — to the 1928 Stanley Cup. In game two of the final series against Montreal, Ranger goalie Lorne Chabot was struck in the eye by a Nels Stewart shot and staggered off for medical treatment. Coach Patrick, long retired from hockey as a player, was forced to don the pads himself after he was refused permission to replace Chabot with a professional substitute. Patrick handled 18 shots, giving up just one goal, and his team won in overtime. The Rangers went on to win the Cup.

Chabot's eye injury was slow to heal and in the off-season there were rumours that his career was over because of failing sight. The Rangers offered him to the Leafs and Conn Smythe jumped at the deal, giving up goalie John Ross Roach in return. Chabot performed admirably for the Leafs for the next three seasons and helped them to win a Stanley Cup in 1932. Oldtimers say he was the first of many great Leaf goaltenders. An oddity of

Chabot's career was that he figured prominently in the two longest games ever played. He was the winning goalie (a 1–0 shutout) in the Leafs' marathon victory over Boston in 1933, a match that went into the sixth overtime period before Ken Doraty scored to end it. Three seasons later, playing for the Montreal Maroons, he was on the losing end of a 1–0 score in a playoff game that lasted 12 minutes longer (116 minutes and 30 seconds of overtime). Detroit's Mud Bruneteau, a two-goal scorer during the regular season, beat him for the winning goal.

It surprised me to learn that Lorne Chabot is not in the Hockey Hall of Fame. He played in the NHL for ten seasons and retired with a total of 73 shutouts and a goals-against average of 2.04. His playoff goals-against average dipped even lower, to 1.50. Compare Chabot's impressive stats with those of other goaltending greats and you find that Turk Broda's goals-against average was 2.53 (1.98 in playoffs) with 62 shutouts, Johnny Bower's goals-against average was 2.52 (2.54 in playoffs) with 37 shutouts, Charlie Rayner finished with a goals-against average of 3.05 (3.57 in playoffs) and 33 shutouts, and Billy Smith's goals-against average was 3.17 (2.73 in playoffs) with 22 shutouts. All of these Hall of Fame netminders, along with others like Gump Worsley, Roy Worters, and Ken Dryden, fail to match Chabot's standards. How come he isn't in the Hall?

Foster's Long Climb

O N opening night, November 12, 1931, and for hundreds of nights afterwards, Foster Hewitt made a long, lonely climb from the bowels of Maple Leaf Gardens up to his broadcasting home, the famous gondola slung 56 feet over centre ice. In the early days Hewitt was the producer, director, play-by-play announcer, and colour commentator — all rolled into one. He lugged a bulky suitcase full of equipment up to his location, and traversed a shaky catwalk that frightened even the most courageous visitors who dared to join him there. One stalwart who failed the test was movie tough guy, actor George Raft. He collapsed in fright on the catwalk and ushers were called upon to assist him down.

As a radio pioneer, and before the construction of the Gardens was finished, Hewitt was allowed to select his own little niche for the broadcasts. If there was an ideal broadcast location he had no idea where it might be. One day Hewitt and one of the building's architects walked down Bay Street to the old Eaton's warehouse. They climbed from floor to floor and looked out over the street at each level. When they got to what they thought would be the best height they were 55 feet above the sidewalk. Foster pictured the pedestrians below as hockey players and thought he could see them well enough to identify them.

Fortuitously one of the main girders in the new arena was 56 feet above ice level and that's where Foster ordered the gondola constructed.

Initially Foster's vivid descriptions of NHL hockey were greeted with mixed feelings around the Gardens. There was a good deal of opposition to his broadcasts for fear they would keep the fans away from the arena. But they turned out to have just the opposite effect. His exciting play-by-play with his famous phrase "He shoots, he scores!" thrilled his listeners and brought the game to thousands of people who became fans. They wanted to see what Foster was describing and they clamoured for tickets. Before long, Foster Hewitt became a bigger celebrity than most of the star players in the game.

Little-Known Facts About the Gardens

DESPITE the swanky ice palaces springing up for hockey all over North America, it will take decades before most of them acquire the heritage of Maple Leaf Gardens, which opened in 1931.

The story of the Gardens' conception, its financing (it cost a paltry $1.5 million), and its contruction in record time (an astonishing six months) is a familiar one to most hockey fans. But some little-known facts about the famous building may be worth revealing. For example:

The first site considered for the new arena was down by the Toronto waterfront, close by Yonge Street. A second site discussed was on Spadina Crescent north of College, but when residents of the area objected, that plan was abandoned.

The T. Eaton Company originally offered Conn Smythe property on Wood Street off Yonge, but Smythe held out for the present site on Church and Carlton because the streetcar lines would be directly in front of his building.

Initially, the ice surface was to run east and west rather than north and south. There was to be a circular gallery installed large enough for 5,000 spectators. The balcony idea was struck before construction got underway.

A gymnasium, a billiard room, and a bowling alley were in the original prospectus. These areas were approved and installed.

Star player and graduate pharmacist Clarence "Hap" Day made a shrewd deal with Mr. Smythe and opened the Hap Day Pharmacy in a corner of the building.

In the cornerstone, laid at the southeast corner of the building, is a manuscript, embedded there on September 21, 1931, by Lieutenant-Governor W. D. Ross. This document records some additional facts about the edifice.

It states that the artificial ice would be manufactured by three 60-ton machines with sufficient capacity to cover the cement floor with ice within eight hours, the ice to be approximately three-quarters of an inch thick.

Into the construction of the building went 750,000 bricks. One bricklayer estimated that, laid end to end, the bricks would stretch from the site to a distance of 28 miles.

The structure required 77,500 bags of cement, 70 tons of sand, 11,000 tons of gravel, 950,000 board feet of lumber, 540 kegs of nails, more than 14 miles of conduit, and over 230,000 haylite blocks. About nine miles of piping was embedded in the cement floor to carry the fluids from the ice-making machines.

The Gardens was an instant success. It was filled to capacity on November 12, 1931, when the Leafs lost the home opener in their new building to Chicago.

One month later not only was it filled again for a unique church service but an estimated 20,000 standing in a drizzle outside had to be turned away.

Not all the Gardens events have been successful but a large variety have been scheduled there. Professional lacrosse, pro basketball, indoor softball, soccer, and dog racing were among the promotional nightmares. One night during the dog races, the mechanical rabbit broke down. The dogs skidded to a halt and wandered off, no doubt in search of hydrants.

On another night the six-day bike racers suspected that the promoters of the event were short of funds. They refused to ride until they were paid in cash.

For a rodeo in the '60s, inches of dirt and straw were laid over the ice surface. But getting the stuff off again in time for a hockey game with Detroit, after the horses had defecated all over it, presented a formidable, time-consuming problem. It was the only NHL game ever played on brown ice.

That was not a night to make Conn Smythe proud, for he insisted from the beginning that the Gardens should be spotlessly clean at all times. There are many bigger, fancier, more glamorous hockey arenas around. But there's no place quite like the Gardens.

The "Busher" Had Everything . . . and Lost It All

H E learned to skate using girls' skates, stumbling around the outdoor ice on Poverty Pond in West Toronto. His skates and sticks were hand-me-downs, discarded by older kids. It was in the early '20s and the kid, like most kids then, learned to cash in pop bottles and hustle newspapers for spending money.

He honed his natural athletic abilities and grew up to be one of the NHL's flashiest performers, a matinee idol with movie-star looks, a player described by Frank Selke as "the classiest player of all time." He was the speediest member of the Leafs' famed "Kid Line" and a five-time league All-Star. His name was Harvey "Busher" Jackson.

As a teenager he helped the Marlboros to three OHA titles and a Memorial Cup triumph in 1929. Soon after, he joined the Leafs. Conn Smythe wisely placed him on a line with Charlie (the Big Bomber) Conacher and (Gentleman) Joe Primeau. The line clicked almost instantly and the "Kid Line" was born. It would become the most famous trio in Leaf history.

Jackson earned his nickname from Leaf trainer Tim Daly. One day the surly trainer asked the Leaf rookie to help carry some sticks to the Leaf bench. "I'm not here to carry sticks," snapped Jackson. "I'm here to play hockey."

Daly snapped back, "Why, you're nothing but a fresh young busher," and the nickname stuck.

In 1932, Jackson celebrated his 21st birthday by winning the NHL scoring title with 28 goals and 25 assists. His 53 points were three more than teammate Primeau and four more than Montreal's Howie Morenz. Jackson became the youngest scoring champion in history. In 1980–81, Wayne Gretzky would win a scoring crown at age 20.

The late Red Burnett, then a young sportswriter for the *Toronto Star*, once said of Jackson,

He had everything — appearance, stickhandling ability, more shifts than a racing car and a blazing backhand shot.

He burst like a roman candle on the NHL scene. Watching Joe Primeau, the clever little center, deal pay-off passes to the giant Charlie Conacher, hurtling down right wing, or Jackson, moving with the grace of a ballet dancer down the left side, is something one never forgets.

The Busher had something special — that extra bit of speed, the size and strength, packed into an almost perfect physique.

Red Dutton, a bashing defenceman with the New York Americans, was awed by Jackson's shift. "He could cut either left or right with an almost perfect fake. He had a knack of weaving past a rearguard so close that he practically brushed sweaters."

Jackson's offensive skills netted him 241 goals during a 15-year career. But the on-ice skills that vaulted him to superstardom were offset by weaknesses away from the arena. An addiction to alcohol and a hunger for the bright lights led to complaints from his hockey bosses, two failed marriages, a series of business failures, and unsuccessful coaching stints. He died too young, at age 55, hobbled in his last few years by a liver ailment and deeply hurt by the fans and cronies who no longer cared about him or had time for him.

I would meet him occasionally in the press room at Maple Leaf Gardens, where he would whisper his need for "a couple of spare bucks." His sallow complexion, shabby clothes, and lined features gave him the appearance of an old man. I recall the occasions he appeared wearing a brace to protect a broken neck suffered in a fall down a flight of stairs. "And I wasn't drinking when it happened," he insisted.

This was the fabulous forward Conn Smythe once described as "priceless." But not so priceless that Smythe didn't shunt him off to the New York Americans in 1940.

Jackson once told me he hoped to see his name in Hockey's Hall of Fame someday despite the well-publicized objections of

Smythe, who carried enough clout with the selection committee to keep him out.

Smythe's argument? "The rules state that candidates for election shall be chosen on the basis of playing ability, integrity, character and their contribution to their team." Obviously, in his opinion, Jackson lacked the character and integrity to be worthy of nomination. In later years, had Smythe stayed around, would he have felt the same way about the induction of Harold Ballard or Alan Eagleson? Or his old friend Jim Norris, who was once investigated for palling around with some underworld figures? Or even NHL president Clarence Campbell, who once served five hours in a Montreal jail cell after being convicted in the Sky Shops scandal?

Smythe once told my colleague Dick Beddoes, "As long as Jackson lives, he must not be admitted to the Hall. If we gave him a Hall of Fame plaque today, he would be on the front steps of the Hall tomorrow — hocking it for booze money." Beddoes argued: "Mr. Smythe, bar him from the Temperance Hall of Fame or even the Chivalry Hall of Fame but for God's sake, not from the Hockey Hall of Fame where performance on the ice should be the important criterion."

Beddoes was echoing sentiments expressed by Jackson's linemate Charlie Conacher: "They inducted Joe and me into the Hall and completely ignored Busher. We should have gone in together — as the Kid Line. That's how we're going to be remembered."

Jackson died in the summer of 1968, his wish unfulfilled. He passed from the scene penniless, bequeathing only a few fading hockey memories.

Five years after his funeral he was finally reunited with his Kid Line comrades in the Hall of Fame. By this time Smythe's protests could be safely ignored. Beddoes wrote a fitting final paragraph: "There is no humanity in an institution which waits five years to salute an individual just to be sure he is very dead. Flowers are worthless unless you are alive to smell them."

Kid Line Overrated, Says Smythe

URING the '30s, the Leaf attack was paced by the famous Kid Line: Conacher, Primeau, and Jackson. They were worshipped by fans from coast to coast — everywhere but in the front office.

Leaf owner Smythe thought the Kid Line was overrated and said so in 1981 when he published his memoirs. "I was a hero worshipper myself," he told ghostwriter Scott Young, "but Jackson wasn't a good enough person to earn the hero worship of kids. That's why I fought for years to keep him out of the Hockey Hall of Fame.

"For all the goals the Kid Line scored, and despite the number of all-star teams they made, as players Conacher and Jackson were never half as good as they were thought to be. They wanted Primeau to do all the work and they'd score all the goals. But you have to play hockey in three spaces: your end, in the neutral zone, and in their end. They didn't do it. But they were an exciting line and the Leafs became one of the highest scoring teams in hockey because of it."

Charlie Conacher's Shot Almost a Killer

IN the early '30s, Charlie Conacher of the Leafs possessed the most feared shot in hockey. There were no sizzling slapshots in those days but Conacher's powerful wrists could send the puck speeding towards, a rival goalie like a rocket. In the final game of the 1932 Stanley Cup playoffs between Toronto and the New York Rangers, Conacher — and over 14,000 fans at Maple Leaf Gardens — feared for the life of Ranger goalie John Ross Roach after he was felled by a Conacher blast.

It happened in the second period of game three, with the Leafs leading 3–1 and the noisy crowd urging the home team on to their third straight win and a Stanley Cup celebration.

Conacher whistled a shot that struck Roach with tremendous force. Here's how Lou Marsh described what happened in the *Toronto Star.*

> It was a period that almost ended in tragedy. Young Chuck Conacher, 205 pounds of TNT, let one of his smoking shots go from away over by the fence just inside the blue line.
>
> Roach, as game as a badger, threw himself in front of the sizzler and it hit him under the heart. The terrific impact drove him back into the nets, but he straightened up again and the puck was cleared.
>
> Then he slowly dropped his stick, struggled a second with his gloved hands at his throat, and silently folded up and dropped to the ice. He looked like a man shot through the heart.
>
> There was a moment's awed silence and then a rippling groan as Roach stiffened out on the ice. It looked as if the popular Port Perry netman had been killed for

he lay without a move.

It was a solar plexus blow — a shock to the big motor centre of the body. It took Roach five minutes to recover.

When Roach staggered back to his feet, Conacher skated over to him. It's reported he said to his rival and old friend, "Don't worry, Johnny. That's the last high shot you'll see from me tonight."

It marked the third time Conacher has knocked a rival player out with his booming shots — and then lowered his sights for fear of killing someone. He kayoed Charlie Gardiner, Chicago netminder, in an earlier playoff game and he knocked out his brother Lionel, who toils on defence for the Maroons. After each injury, he laid off any high drives from the rest of the game.

Charlie Conacher won the NHL scoring title twice and was the league's top goal scorer in four of his big-league seasons. He wore number 9 and made it the most coveted number in the game. He scored 225 goals in his career. His brother Roy, much less flamboyant, collected 226 goals.

Doraty Ends Torrid Grind

ON April Fool's Day, 1933, a record crowd filled Maple Leaf Gardens for the fifth and deciding game of the semifinal series between Boston and Toronto. Every windowsill in the building was packed with S.R.O. spectators. Some brought folding camp chairs to stand on. Others rented soft-drink boxes. A few "borrowed" cuspidors from the men's rooms, turned them upside down, and stood on them. Anything to elevate themselves a few inches in order to see over the heads of others and watch the thrilling action below. When the attendance record was announced — 14,539 — many said it would stand forever.

At the end of the amazing marathon, no one complained they didn't get their money's worth, for the spine-tingling struggle would enter the history books as an epic, a playoff game like no other ever witnessed.

The *Toronto Star*, in bold print, offered a concise synopsis of the action in its next edition:

Ken Doraty Comes Through With Lone Goal After Record Crowd Had Sat Through 164.46 Minutes of Scoreless Hockey — Fans in a Frenzy as Toronto Team Triumphs in Nerve-Wracking Playoff Game — Players Troop Off Ice in State of Exhaustion — Winners En Route to Meet Rangers in Stanley Cup Finals — Andy Blair Combines With Syracuse Rookie for Million Dollar Tally — Struggle Will Go Down as Greatest in History of Professional Hockey — Conquerors Proved Themselves Men of Mettle.

At exactly 8:30 p.m. referees Daigneault and Cleghorn brought the teams to centre ice for the opening faceoff. At 1:48 the following morning, in the sixth period of overtime, the fans rocked Conn Smythe's new ice palace to its very foundations with a salvo of cheering as little Ken Doraty whipped the puck past Bruin goaltender Tiny Thompson for the only goal of the game. Until that moment, Thompson had been sensational and had faced 114 shots. His counterpart, Lorne Chabot in the Toronto goal, had faced 93 shots and stopped them all.

Blair and Doraty were two unlikely heroes. Doraty, one of the smallest players in hockey at 124 pounds, had recently been called up from Syracuse to replace Dave Downie. In a previous trial it was said that Doraty lacked endurance and simply wouldn't make the grade in the NHL. Blair, it was reported, was at the end of his career following a recent injury.

For 164 minutes and 46 seconds the teams, comprising some of the greatest players the world of hockey has ever known, battled each other into a state of exhaustion. They were travel-weary, dragging one skate after another, while the fans were physically exhausted. After the fifth overtime period had been played, some players wanted to stop. But a conference with NHL President Frank Calder resulted in the decree: "Play to a finish!"

It was suggested that a coin be flipped, with the lucky guesser gaining the championship. And the teams actually paraded on the ice to witness the coin flip that never happened. "Let's play without goalies, that should settle things in a hurry," was another proposal that was vetoed by Calder. It's a wonder a shootout wasn't proposed, similar to the tiebreakers that are employed in modern-day hockey.

The goat of the contest was Bruin immortal Eddie Shore, the highest-paid and most-feared defenceman in hockey. Shore's cross-ice pass was intercepted by Blair. He threw a quick pass to Doraty, who took a couple of choppy strides towards Thompson, fired the puck, and scored!

Hats flew out on the ice. Programs fluttered down. The crowd was delirious with delight. Before his mates could leap on Doraty's toothpick-slim frame, he dove into the net and retrieved the puck, souvenir of the greatest athletic feat he would ever perform. His mates hugged and kissed him and dragged him back to the bench. One Leaf — Harold Cotton — skated around the ice kicking hats into the air. He fell down, got up, and did an Irish jig. He pulled a battered derby over his head and made comical faces at the fans.

Boston coach Art Ross took the devastating loss like a champion. He embraced Leaf defenceman King Clancy and planted a kiss on his cheek. Earlier in the season, during a dispute in Boston, a snarling Ross had tried to plant another kind of kiss on Clancy — using his knuckles.

The following day, Lou Marsh, esteemed sports editor of the *Toronto Star*, wrote of Doraty's delightful deed and was widely criticized by his readers for his comments. Marsh wrote in part:

> **The gink who always breaks up these epic hockey matches is always some meek and lowly punk . . . some comparative nonentity who comes from behind the bar-**

rel to carve his name on the tablets of athletic fame.

The gent with the ready roscoe who broke up last night's titanic struggle was the midget of the team — Ken Doraty . . . little undersized runt as far as big league hockey players go . . . lightest and smallest player on the roster . . . the kid who hauls down the thinnest envelope . . . last sub on the relief corps . . . the tool the mastermind uses when all others are blunted.

Now get me right — I don't intend to insinuate that Ken Doraty, who played the hero's role last night, is literally a punk. He is a gallant and game young man, but he is just plain lucky to be on the Leaf payroll!

And yet he stepped through with the million dollar goal of the game of a million thrills . . . crashed the front page with his photo in double columns . . . same size as the editor would give an assassinated prince . . . a general who won the war . . . or a president who turned the banking system of his country upside down.

Who is this overnight hero of the hockey world?

He was born right here in Ontario . . . in a burg most of you don't even know . . . Stittsville . . . a bulge in the highway down in Carleton county . . . somewhere near Ottawa . . . one of those burgs hardly big enough to have a local correspondent for the nearest town paper.

Went out to Regina with his folks . . . first came into hockey prominence with the Regina Pats in 1925 . . . played with Portland out on the coast . . . came to the Chicago Blackhawks in the NHL . . . back to Minneapolis . . . down this way with the Kitcheners . . . Toronto Millionaires out at Ravina rink . . . and Cleveland Indians in the International League . . . then to Syracuse of the same league . . . and now the hero of the NHL season.

For the next few weeks Marsh fended off fans and harsh letters. His critics objected to his use of the words "punk" and "undersized runt" to describe the 27-year-old Doraty. One of them described himself as "not much bigger than Doraty myself. And nobody calls me a runt!"

Ken Doraty ended the longest game ever played at Maple Leaf Gardens, a game preceding by three years one in Montreal between Detroit and the Maroons that would last a dozen minutes or so longer.

But Doraty had no time to celebrate his feat. After the game the Leafs rushed to board a special train that took them to New York and the first game of the final series, scheduled for the following night. Apparently no one questioned the unfairness of such an arrangement. The Leafs arrived late in the afternoon and, staggering with fatigue, were completely outclassed by the Rangers and lost the opener 5–1. In game two Doraty scored the lone Toronto goal in a 3–1 Ranger victory, and collected two more goals in game three, won by the Leafs 3–2. Bill Cook scored the only goal in game four — an overtime marker — and the Rangers captured the Stanley Cup.

Doraty stayed with Toronto for the next two seasons and scored another 10 goals in 45 games.

A fascinating postscript: During the following season, Doraty established a record that can never be broken. When Toronto met Ottawa on January 16, 1934, the game was tied 4–4 at the end of regulation time. The overtime rule in that era required a full 10 minutes of extra play — no sudden-death endings. Doraty rattled in three goals in the overtime frame and the Leafs won the contest 7–4. He thus became the only player ever to score a hat trick in overtime.

Leafs Missed Boat on Mighty Milt

BOSTON Bruin legend Milt Schmidt, one of the best centremen ever to play in the NHL, almost became a Maple Leaf. It was only the personal bias of Leaf owner Conn Smythe that kept Schmidt from joining such immortal Toronto pivots in the '40s as Ted Kennedy, Syl Apps, and Max Bentley.

Smythe's assistant Frank Selke, before his death in 1985, revealed that he was all set to sign Schmidt to a Leaf contract in the mid-1930s — for a bonus of $250. Both men were from Kitchener, Ontario, and Selke figured the 18-year-old was destined for NHL stardom. But Selke was under instructions from Smythe to get his approval before spending money on young hopefuls.

"When I mentioned Schmidt's name, Smythe's reaction was astonishing," Selke would say. "He told me to forget about him. There's no place for a goddamn squarehead (a person of German extraction) on my team," said Smythe. He had fought in World War I and would march again in the second great conflict. He disliked Germans with a passion. So Selke was forced to break off negotiations with Schmidt and could only think of what might have been when the youngster signed with Boston a short time later — for $3,000.

Smythe's prejudice wasn't only against Germans. He once told Toronto native Herb Carnegie, the best black player in the world in the '40s, "I'd sign you in a minute if I could turn you white."

Milt Schmidt went on to centre the famous "Kraut Line" in Boston, with Woody Dumart and Bobby Bauer on the wings. He scored 229 goals during his career, winning the scoring crown in

1940 and the Hart Trophy in 1952. He was inducted into the Hockey Hall of Fame in 1961.

Lionel Conacher Was a Canny Foe

LIONEL Conacher, Canada's Athlete of the Half-Century, excelled in all sports — football, baseball, lacrosse, boxing, and hockey. Because of his boxing prowess, when hockey fights broke out he was a man to be avoided.

One night Conacher's Montreal Maroons were playing the Leafs at Maple Leaf Gardens. A brawl erupted involving all of the players from both teams. When the Leafs' Bob Davidson looked around, the only opposing player without a partner was Conacher. Davidson grabbed the big defenceman by the shirt and pinned him up against the boards. Davidson wrestled Conacher for a minute or two, and was pleased to see his hard work was paying off, for Conacher could not squirm loose to throw any of his devastating punches.

Suddenly Conacher relaxed. Nodding at the players milling about behind Davidson, he said, "It's all over, kid. Fight's all finished. Now let me go, willyah?" Davidson did.

With lightning speed, Conacher threw a short right hand. It exploded in Davidson's face, knocking him bow-legged.

"I can't believe he suckered me like that," Davidson said later.

Smythe Starts Riot in Beantown

O
N March 16, 1932, Toronto Maple Leaf manager Conn Smythe triggered a small riot at the Boston Garden after the home-town Bruins scored three goals against his team — all of them tallied with Leaf goalie Lorne Chabot sitting in the penalty box!

In the first few minutes of play, Chabot prevented a goal by tripping Bruin star Cooney Weiland, who was buzzing around his net. Referee Bill Stewart, a Boston native and grandfather of current NHL ref Paul Stewart, handed Chabot a two-minute penalty and ordered him to the penalty box. In that era, penal-ties to goaltenders were usually costly, simply because the men in the big pads had to serve their own penalty time. Chabot was surprised by the call because not one NHL netminder had been penalized all season; he was the first. The call infuriated Conn Smythe, who leaped from his seat on the Leaf bench and casti-gated Stewart with a dose of criticism that could be heard throughout the Boston Garden. Smythe was further incensed when the Bruins fired three pucks into the Leaf net against three different substitute netminders — none wearing goal pads — while Chabot squirmed on the penalty bench. First, Alex Levin-sky gave up a goal to the Bruins' Marty Barry. Then Red Horner replaced Levinsky and promptly allowed a second goal by Barry. King Clancy, who had once played goal for Ottawa under similar circumstances in a Stanley Cup game and was not scored on, then grabbed the goal stick away from Horner, only to meet with a fate similar to his porous teammates'. He fanned on a George Owen shot.

By then Smythe was enraged. When referee Stewart skated close to the Leaf bench, Smythe leaned over the boards and tried to grab him by the sweater. This didn't surprise Stewart, for Smythe had a reputation for grabbing at game officials.

Sometimes he ran out on the ice after them. Stewart skidded to a stop and immediately ordered the Leaf owner off the bench. To make sure his orders were carried out, the referee called upon four burly Boston policemen to handle the situation.

But Smythe refused to leave and a small riot broke out while the Boston fans hooted and jeered Smythe and his players. The Leafs grouped around Smythe while he argued with Stewart and told the coppers to back off. Several fans moved in, and when one loudmouth threatened Smythe, Leaf player Harold Cotton threw a wild punch at the man. Cotton was about to unleash several more blows, when his mates grabbed him and held him back.

After several minutes of heated discussion and some pushing and shoving, Smythe was escorted from the Leaf bench while the fans hurled their programs and jeered his departure. No one was happier to see the little colonel's dilemma than Boston manager Art Ross, Smythe's longtime hockey nemesis.

The three quick goals by the Bruins against the three perplexed and padless Leaf substitute goaltenders were too big a margin to overcome and Boston marched off with a 6–2 victory.

The following appeared in the *Toronto Star* the next day:

The NHL should keep a penalty list for managers and coaches. If they did, Conny Smythe, the fiery Toronto leader, would be the "Ching Johnson" or the "Red Dutton" of the group! Cornelius was run off the bench again last night — this time in Boston. That is the second time he has been ordered "to the showers" this season.

———————

Referee Bill Stewart was also a major league baseball umpire. In 1937 he was hired to coach the Chicago Blackhawks and he guided them to a surprising Stanley Cup triumph in 1938. He was the toast of Chicago for a few months. Then the owner fired him.

Another Smart Move

IN the spring of 1932, the Leafs and the New York Rangers hooked up in a game at Maple Leaf Gardens and the Leafs managed to win 5–3. But the big story of the game was a "fast one" pulled by Conn Smythe and coach Dick Irvin. Lou Marsh, sports editor of the *Toronto Star,* saw it this way:

> It was the smartest move I've seen around here since the day (coach) Ed Wildey yanked his goalkeeper out in a junior game and sent out six forwards to pull a lost game out of the grate. I'm gabbing about the smart move — the tricky move — the smart eggs behind the Maple Leaf bench pulled in the last second of last night's game with New York.
>
> What did they do? They deliberately had Charlie Conacher and Red Horner (two injured Leaf stars) commit offenses which brought them their third majors — and automatic suspension for one game!
>
> Wha-a — Whafor?
>
> Let me repeat it. The Maple Leaf masterminds deliberately arranged to have Conacher and Horner commit offenses which brought them their third majors — and automatic suspension for one game.
>
> Go ahead and ask your questions! I did myself.
>
> Conacher and Horner were thrown on the ice in the last five seconds of the game last night before the men they were relieving were off the pond — in order that they might get their third major fouls and be automatically suspended for one game. Because both were on the crippled list and both had already collected two major fouls this season, it had been shrewdly figured out that they would best serve suspensions NOW, while they were useless to the club. They'd be ready — with clean sheets — to step into the playoffs.

In the heat of the playdowns, since both men are full of dynamite and razor blades, it was thought likely they'd draw another major — and the one game automatic suspension. That might ruin Leafs' chances in a battling playoff. Now they have their "thirds" — and their suspensions — behind them and the Leafs will have plenty of elbow room in the playoff jamboree.

Smart, wasn't it?

How was it worked?

Simple enough. The two cripples were dressed and when the clock said five seconds to play, they jumped out on the ice. The referees rang their bells and for once found two gladiators pleading for a term in "the big house."

The two the fixers failed to fix were Bill Long and Bill Christie, the penalty timekeepers. In his excitement, Bill Long, who is valet to the Big Ben that hangs over the middle of the arena and does everything but referee the game, let the clock run on and the clock showed "time up" before the referees could untangle themselves and get the yearning prisoners into the penalty box.

Christie almost turned a back flip when he saw Conacher and Horner clambering over the boards and tried to argue the bell ringers into giving them only a minor penalty as they do in amateur hockey for such dastardly crimes.

But the referees knew their cues. They bowed Chuck and Red into the calaboose, faced the puck off at centre ice and the game was over. The crowd sat around and wondered what it was all about.

Smart idea?

Yep! But some other fellows will probably call it skullduggery and demand that President Calder erase the major penalties imposed and suspend the suspensions.

Trickery has no place in sport — that is ordinarily speaking — but here is one case where most of the folks will be inclined to support a tricky move.

Personally — if that counts with you — I'd like to see

the Leafs get away with this stark, wide-open piece of sports trickery simply because the rule which automatically suspends a player for three major fouls is a bit of utter nonsense. Every foul should stand on its own merits. As it is now one player can deliberately cut down a rival and unless they send for the ambulance or the coroner he doesn't get anything more than a chap who trips a man to save a goal — and not half as much as the chap who intimates that the referee's nearest female relative barks or is inclined to have fleas.

Toronto Teams Make History, Win All Three Major Championships

IN the spring of 1932, for the first time in hockey history, Toronto hockey teams held the Stanley, the Allan, and the Memorial Cup championships. In a postseason banquet at the Royal York Hotel, the Maple Leafs, winners of the Stanley Cup, the National Sea Fleas, holders of the Allan Cup, and the Marlboros, Junior A champions of Canada, were honoured for distinguishing themselves on the ice. The players went home laden down with gifts of all descriptions.

The Marlboros received the J. Ross Robertson junior trophy. The players received OHA medals and crests and gold watches and chains from the Marlboro club. As senior amateur champions, the Nationals were presented with the Allan Cup and the J. Ross Robertson senior trophy. Individual players received medals and crests from the CAHA and the OHA. Mayor Stewart of Toronto also presented them with wristwatches on behalf of the city.

The Maple Leafs received the Stanley Cup, and the individual members were presented with an illuminated scroll from Mayor Stewart. The Ontario Athletic Commission presented the Leafs with travelling sets and a local firm gave them belts and suspenders.

The most prized gift received by the Leafs was a gold medal presented by Chairman Bickell to each player on behalf of the directors, entitling the holder to a lifetime pass to Maple Leaf Gardens at any time and for any attraction.

Not to be outdone, the players then presented manager Conn Smythe with a split-second watch with which to time the trials of his new thoroughbred horses — Six-to-Four, Stanley Cup, and Three Straight. All the names reflected on the recent series won by the Leafs in three straight games by identical 6–4 scores.

All three championship trophies were on display for several days in the window of Eaton's College Street store.

Toronto Player Chooses Wedding March over Victory Parade

IN mid-April of 1932, the Chicago Shamrocks of the American Hockey League were on the verge of winning the league championship. One more playoff victory over the Duluth Hornets and they'd be able to break out the champagne.

Prior to the biggest game of the season, Chicago manager Babe Dye, a former Toronto hockey star, received an unusual request from Gordon Brydson, his team captain.

"Boss, I hate to tell you this but I've made wedding plans back in Toronto and the date coincides with the date of the game with Duluth. I want your permission to skip the game so that I can keep the wedding date."

Dye was astonished. In all his career as a player and coach, he'd never heard of such a request. Reluctantly, he gave his star player permission to leave. Perhaps he concluded that a wedding requires greater priority than a hockey game, even a championship match. Possibly he gleaned that Brydson was ready to declare himself wedding-bound with or without the coach's sanction. So he gave his approval and stood by while Brydson called his fiancée, Miss Dorothy Beamish, and told her, "Good news, honey. I'm coming home."

One can imagine the reaction of the team owner, Thomas Shaughnessy, when he was told his prize rooster had fled the coop. He asked Dye if he knew that Brydson was headed home and Dye admitted that he did.

"Then you're fired," roared Shaughnessy. He also fired the team publicity director and announced that Brydson the bridegroom was suspended immediately and indefinitely.

The Toronto papers sided with Shaughnessy. The *Toronto Star* editorialized:

Babe Dye certainly pulled a prize boner when he gave Gord Brydson, captain of his team, permission to jump his club when they were in the middle of a championship series. The player left for the purpose of getting married. Brydson might easily have postponed his musical march down the aisle, but the league could hardly be expected to postpone a final game for the convenience of one player. Nor could the owners of the club be expected to smile sweetly when the captain of the team slipped away and left the club flat in the middle of the titular series. The drastic action taken by president Shaughnessy in releasing Dye outright and suspending Brydson seems quite justified.

Dye was a great favourite with the Chicago fans and was regarded as one of the chief drawing cards of the team. During the season, Shaughnessy had shown his appreciation of Dye's splendid work by having his picture painted at one end of the Coliseum, the Shamrocks' home rink. Now it's a case of "page the whitewasher" for it's a cinch the masterpiece will have small chance of retaining its proud position at the end of the rink.

This little drama wouldn't be complete without revealing the end of the story. Despite the desertion of their star player, and the dismissal of their coach, the Shamrocks scored a dramatic overtime victory over Duluth in the third and final game of the championship series.

By then, Brydson was looking forward, not only to his honeymoon, but also to his new job as a golf professional at the Mississauga Golf Club in Port Credit, Ontario.

Leaf Goalie Sparkles on NHL's First Penalty Shot

FOR the 1934–35 hockey season, the NHL introduced something new: the penalty shot. And it was diminutive Leaf goalie George Hainsworth who faced the first one. On November 10, 1934, at Maple Leaf Gardens, Montreal's Armand Mondou was awarded the history-making free shot, and missed a chance for immortality when little George turned aside his scoring attempt. It turned out to be a crucial save, for the Leafs went on to edge the Habs 2–1.

Two nights later Ralph (Scotty) Bowman of the St. Louis Eagles scored the first penalty shot goal in NHL history when he beat Montreal's Alex Connell. (No, he's no relation to Scotty Bowman the coach.) It was one of three goals Bowman scored in 43 games that season, and his historic marker was one of only four successful penalty shots out of 29 awarded.

George Hainsworth played in 465 regular season games in the NHL (for the Montreal Canadiens and the Toronto Maple Leafs) and turned in some astonishing numbers. He recorded 49 shutouts in his first three seasons (1926–29), 22 of them in 44 games in 1928–29, which remains a single-season record. He was given his outright release by the Leafs (Smythe didn't like him much) in 1937, after compiling 91 shutouts and a career goals-against average of 2.02. During his 22-shutout season he gave up a mere 43 goals in 44 games, for a minuscule goals-against average of 0.98.

Pass Me the Puck!

IN the '30s, Leaf star Harold "Baldy" Cotton allowed his frustration with his teammates to get the better of him one night. During a game, Cotton found himself in the clear several times but the puck never once came his way. "Dammit, why don't they pass me the puck," he grumbled, loud enough for some of his mates to overhear.

Before the next contest, a road game in New York, he announced that he'd had enough. "If you fellows won't pass the puck to me, then I won't be passing it to any of you," he declared. "Two can play at that little game."

Tough Charlie Conacher thought he could change Cotton's mind and knew just how to do it. It would be unorthodox but effective.

The team was cloistered high up in a Manhattan hotel, 20 floors above Broadway, and Conacher recalled that Cotton had once expressed a fear of heights. When Cotton moved close to an open window, Conacher grabbed him from behind, dropped him over the window ledge headfirst, and held him securely by the ankles. Clancy once told me Cotton's screams startled a herd of cows munching grass in a field in New Jersey, and Clancy was never one to exaggerate.

"What'd you say about not passing the puck to me and the boys?" barked strongman Conacher.

"I didn't mean it, Charlie. Honest. Just let me back in the room," pleaded his terrified teammate.

Conacher hauled the ashen-faced Cotton in, patted him on the back, and said, "That's more like it, Harold. And we'll try and give you a pass once in a while, too."

Harold Cotton played with Pittsburgh for the first four years of his NHL career and scored just 25 goals over that span. Traded to the Leafs, he almost equalled his previous output in his first season with Toronto, scoring 21 times. He played six years for the Leafs and wound up his career with a two-season stint in New York with the Americans. He scored 101 career goals in 500 games. In retirement he became a scout for the Boston Bruins and was a longtime member of the Hot Stove League, a popular intermission feature of *Hockey Night in Canada* on network radio.

Ace Bailey's Final Game

ACE Bailey was a superb left winger for the Leafs in the late '20s and early '30s. Despite a career shortened by a near-fatal incident on December 12, 1933, Bailey's solid work earned him induction into the Hockey Hall of Fame in 1975.

It was King Clancy who first gave me an eyewitness account of the "Ace Bailey incident." Another who watched in horror from near the Leaf bench that night was Frank Selke. Later, just before his death, Bailey himself added additional details, even though he remembered little of the bodycheck that wrote *finis* to his career. Here's what happened that night at the Boston Garden.

The Bruins' defenceman Eddie Shore led a Boston rush toward the Leaf zone but he was tripped up by Clancy at the blue line. Shore slid along the ice and waited for the referee to wave Clancy

The 1927–28 Leafs: (back row) Patterson, Primeau, Smith, Smythe, Gross, Cox, Daly; (front row) Day, Ramsay, Carson, Roach, McCaffery, Bailey, Keeling.
— Hockey Hall of Fame

In 1932, Busher Jackson, barely 21, won the NHL scoring title with 28 goals and 25 assists.
— Hockey Hall of Fame

A near-fatal collision with Eddie Shore of the Bruins abruptly ended Ace Bailey's hockey career with the Leafs.
— Bill Galloway

Foster Hewitt at the microphone on Ace Bailey night.
— Public Archives of Canada/C29556

In the early '30s, Charlie Conacher possessed the most feared shot in hockey. — Hockey Hall of Fame

On April 1, 1933, the Leafs' Ken Doraty finally beat the Boston goalie, after 164:46 minutes of scoreless hockey. — Hockey Hall of Fame

On November 10, 1934, George Hainsworth stopped the NHL's first penalty shot, attempted by Montreal's Armand Mondou.
— Hockey Hall of Fame

The Leafs face the Bruins on an opening night at the Gardens in the '30s.
— Hockey Hall of Fame

Fans line up for tickets in the early days of Maple Leaf Gardens. — Hockey Hall of Fame

The famous Kid Line: Conacher, Primeau, and Jackson. — Hockey Hall of Fame

Harold (Baldy) Cotton played six years with the Leafs; later he became a scout for the Bruins.
— Michael Burns Photography

Trainer Tim Daly flanked by Charlie Conacher (left) and Ted Kennedy in their Sunday best.
— Hockey Hall of Fame

Left to right: Gus Marker, Billy Taylor, and Sweeney Schriner. — Hockey Hall of Fame

Coach Hap Day and Major Conn Smythe in the Leafs' dressing room. — Hockey Hall of Fame

Smythe broke up the Blackhawks' feared Pony Line in 1947 by trading five Leafs for star centre Max Bentley.
— Hockey Hall of Fame

Potential Leafs Mair, Sloan, Cuts, Samis, and Barbe get ready for the start of the 1947–48 season. — Hockey Hall of Fame

Walter (Turk) Broda watches as fellow Leafs battle the New York Rangers.
— Hockey Hall of Fame

Leaf captain Ted Kennedy led his team to five Stanley Cup victories.
— Hockey Hall of Fame

A jubilant coach Joe Primeau hangs on to his hat. — Hockey Hall of Fame

Leaf Bill Barilko's 1951 Stanley Cup–winning goal in sudden-death overtime.
— Hockey Hall of Fame

Barilko's teammates leap off the bench at Maple Leaf Gardens to celebrate his goal.
— Hockey Hall of Fame

off with a penalty. When no penalty was called, Shore rose to his feet, glowering. By this time Clancy was leading a return rush and was deep in Boston territory, fighting for possession of the puck. Ace Bailey, with his back to Shore, dropped back to the blue line to cover for Clancy. Shore wheeled up behind the unsuspecting Bailey, and whether he mistook him for Clancy or not has never been made clear. Shore charged into Bailey from the rear, striking him with such force that Bailey was thrown into the air, his body somersaulting backwards.

The players on both teams, most of the fans, and the men high in the press box heard a crack that might be compared to the sound of smacking a pumpkin with a baseball bat. Bailey's head hit the ice and he lay on his back as though his neck were broken. His legs, bent at the knees, began twitching.

Red Horner, who was on the ice playing for Toronto, rushed up to Shore and snarled, "Why the hell did you do that, Eddie?"

When Shore just grinned, Horner threw a punch that struck his jaw and knocked him cold. Shore's head cracked on the ice and he lay in a rapidly expanding pool of blood. Both injured players were carried off the ice unconscious.

Conn Smythe tried to make his way to the dressing room — it was actually the room used by the Bruins' minor league team, the Cubs — to check on Bailey's condition. En route he was punched by a fan. Smythe punched back. Just then Clancy raced over, brandishing a hockey stick. "Don't touch my boss," screamed Clancy.

Bailey came around in the small room and for a few seconds he appeared to be all right. Tim Daly, the team trainer, offered encouragement: "Come on, Ace," he said. "You'll be back in the game. You got a bump on the head, is all. I've seen lots worse in the prize ring."

Bailey tried to get up, then slumped back. Dr. Kelley, the Bruins' team doctor, arrived and began to examine Bailey. He said, "Get an ambulance here fast!" He turned to Daly and added softly, "If this young man is a Roman Catholic, someone should call a priest immediately."

While the ambulance was on its way, Eddie Shore, having recovered somewhat from Horner's knockout blow, and with 16 stitches in his scalp, came into the room and apologized to the groggy Bailey.

Bailey is reported to have slurred a response through trembling lips. "That's all right, Eddie. It's all part of the game."

It was an eternity before the ambulance arrived. In fact the game was over when Bailey was finally taken to the hospital. His mates left for the train station. They had a game to play in Montreal two nights later.

Fortunately, in Boston at that time there were two neurosurgeons who were particularly skilled in dealing with Bailey's type of injury. Two delicate operations were performed seven days apart. Internal damage was so severe that the surgeons offered little hope for his survival. Smythe began making arrangements to have Bailey's body shipped back to Toronto. The doctors had told him his star player couldn't possibly make it. But Bailey's fighting spirit was a factor they might have overlooked, and certainly he was in the best possible physical condition to submit to major surgery. While his teammates and family held their breath, Bailey fought for his life. On one occasion a nurse on duty rushed in to save his life when he swallowed his tongue.

One nurse took a particular interest in Bailey. Hour after hour she held his hand and urged him not to quit: "Keep fighting, Ace. Everybody is praying for you."

It was true. All across Canada fans were praying for his recovery. Thousands of get-well cards arrived at the Boston hospital. There was a nationwide sigh of relief when it was announced, "The crisis is over. Bailey is on his way to recovery."

Ace was quick to credit Dr. Munro, one of the Boston neurosurgeons, for keeping him on the planet. Bailey told me in 1990, a few months before he passed away,

It was Dr. Munro who saved my life. He drilled a hole in each side of my skull. There was a life-threatening blood clot in there between the brain and the skull. He went to work and sucked that clot out of there. Took him two and a half hours to get it all because it came out in pieces. He told me he was ready for a large glass of brandy when he was done.

I was going to press charges against Shore and the Bruins but Dr. Munro advised me against it. He said, "Ace, you may get only $5,000 or so if you win a lawsuit. But I hear they're going to hold a benefit game for you in Toronto and you'll get a lot more money from that than you will by going to court." So I withdrew the charges.

Dr. Munro let me come home to Toronto and a few weeks later I got a letter from the Boston Bruins. Guess what was inside? It was a cheque for $7,800, part of the gate receipts from a game between the Bruins and the Maroons. With that money we bought some property and built a house on it. It cost us exactly $7,800. Try doing that today. Then, when they held the big benefit game for me at Maple Leaf Gardens, we received another cheque — this one for about $20,000. That money was placed in a trust company and they sent us a cheque every month for years.

It was during the Toronto game — forerunner to the annual All-Star game — that Bailey and Shore met again, at centre ice. When Shore offered his hand and Bailey took it, indicating there were no hard feelings, the crowd erupted in a tremendous ovation.

"I was never the type of man to hold grudges — against anybody," Bailey told me. "With my dad, it wasn't quite the same story. My dad, after listening to a description of my injury on the radio, became distraught. Within hours he left Toronto and headed for Boston — packing a loaded gun. He vowed not to return until he'd shot the man who'd nearly killed me. Fortunately Conn Smythe and Frank Selke got wind of it and took care of the situation."

Frank Selke, who had returned to Toronto with the Leafs after the Bailey-Shore incident, received a phone call from Conn Smythe in Boston.

"Frank, Ace Bailey's dad is here and the word is he's out to get Shore. Threatens to shoot him. Can you do something about this situation?"

Selke could and did. He contacted an old friend, Bob Huddy, a former Boston policeman, and gave him the name of the hotel in which he could find Bailey. Huddy went to the hotel, located Bailey in the bar, and befriended him. After several drinks, Bailey showed Huddy the gun he'd brought with him from Toronto. "With this weapon I'll soon make Shore regret he injured my son," vowed Bailey.

Huddy took the gun and persuaded Bailey to walk with him to the train station. There he put Bailey aboard a train bound for Canada, flashed his badge, and told the conductor to make sure the old fellow stayed on the train until it arrived back in Toronto.

Bailey's career over, Conn Smythe hired him as a minor official for games at Maple Leaf Gardens, and he was a fixture there for the next 47 years. Harold Ballard dismissed him before he reached the half-century mark and Bailey remained bitter about it for the rest of his life. "I didn't even get a thank-you note from Ballard for all those years I put in," he complained. "Others did when they were let go, but not me. I saw the letters signed by Ballard and I told him about it once. He said, 'Ace, I didn't send any letters.' I said, 'Oh yes you did. I saw your signature on them.' He said, 'Not my signature. One of my staff must have signed it.' I said, 'Harold, I know your handwriting and it was your signature.' He snarled, 'Okay, then I lied to you.' And I said, 'Thanks for admitting it. Now you can take this job and stuff it up your keister.'"

A Gift Goal for Convey

EDDIE Convey was a 1930s hockey player whose skills never quite matched those of his pals in the game, men like Charlie Conacher, Red Horner, and King Clancy. After a tryout with the Leafs, Convey was sent to the minors and was later sold to the New York Rangers.

With the Rangers he played game after game without scoring, and word reached his friends in Toronto that he'd soon be back in the minors if he didn't start beating goalies now and again.

Clancy, Horner, and Conacher came up with a scheme to help their old buddy. Clancy said, "Fellows, Convey's playing against us tonight. If we get a good lead in the game, let's see if we can't make him look good out there."

By the end of the second period the Leafs were in front by three or four goals, and Clancy instructed his mates during the intermission. "In the third period, when Convey gets the puck, let him breeze by you on the wing, Charlie. Then Horner and I will lunge at him and miss and maybe he'll score on Chabot."

He called Chabot over. "Lorne, we want Convey to get a goal tonight. It could keep him in the league. If he comes in on you, give him lots of open net. Know what I mean?" Chabot nodded and said he'd do his part.

Sure enough, early in the third period, Convey made a dash down the boards, slipped by Conacher, zipped in between Clancy and Horner, and broke in on goal. When Chabot sprawled awkwardly, Convey drilled a hard shot — that sailed high over the net!

"He sure screwed that up," grumbled Conacher as the players gathered around Chabot.

"I gave him the whole net," said Chabot. "Now what'll we do?"

"We've got to give him another chance," said Clancy.

Again Convey snared the puck and raced in. Left Conacher in his wake. Breezed past Clancy's lunge. Darted in on Chabot, who dropped to the ice, leaving the upper part of the net wide open. Convey muscled a shot that sailed up . . . up . . . and struck Chabot right in the Adam's apple.

Chabot was left writhing on the ice, gasping for breath through a bruised throat, while his three conspirators gathered around.

Finally the goalie croaked, "That's it! Friend or not, next time that son of a bitch comes down cut his bleepin' legs from under him."

When I assisted Clancy with his autobiography in 1968, he wouldn't let me use the above story in the book. His friend Convey was still living then and Clancy was afraid it might embarrass him. As for Convey, in 36 NHL games spread over three seasons, he scored one goal.

A Night for the King

BACK in the mid-'60s, when I was trying to drum up enough courage to write my first hockey book, I prevailed upon King Clancy to sit down with me and record some of his favourite hockey yarns for posterity. The conversations, recorded on tape, now repose in the National Archives in Ottawa, there for future hockey historians to discover and enjoy.

Here are a couple of them, told in the inimitable Clancy style.

Whenever I think back to March 17, 1934, and recall how the Toronto Maple Leafs honoured me with a "night" on St. Patrick's Day, I get a lump in my throat. Remember, I wasn't a native son. I'd played nine years with the Ottawa Senators before coming to Toronto.

Even so, they paid me the greatest tribute any hockey player could ever hope to get. I didn't do anything to deserve it. I figure they just got together and said, "Why not give the old Irishman a night?"

How could I ever forget it? Can you believe they talked me into getting dressed in a green uniform with a big white shamrock stitched on the back? They had me wear a long white beard and somebody placed a crown on my head. A huge crowd filled the Gardens that night to see the pre-game shenanigans and a nasty game that followed against the New York Rangers.

First they brought Mr. Smythe to the microphone, supposedly to introduce me, but he kept getting interrupted by a batch of telegrams announcing my impending arrival.

The Rangers were good sports and joined in the fun. Their big defenceman Ching Johnson hauled a huge float onto the ice in the shape of a potato. The crowd was sure I was inside the float. But they were fooled when it opened up and some Junior "B" players from St. Mike's flew out.

Then a lot of other floats appeared and I wasn't in any of those either. One of my teammates, Ken Doraty — he's the little guy who scored the winning goal in the longest game ever played at Maple Leaf Gardens, in the sixth overtime period against Boston — well, he came out of a large pipe and Harold Cotton popped out of a huge top hat. Our trainer, Tim Daly, was hidden in a big bottle of ginger ale and goalie George Hainsworth emerged from inside a big boot. Red Horner, the team tough guy, stepped out of a giant boxing glove, which was appropriate, and Gentleman Joe Primeau came out of a harp of all things.

When a big shamrock showed up, the crowd roared because they thought I was inside it. But Bill Cook, a great Ranger star, stepped out and took a bow.

When my turn finally came, the lights in the building were dimmed. Then, wearing my royal robes, my crown, and my scraggly beard, I was ushered in on a makeshift throne, pulled along the ice by my pal Hap Day. When the float reached centre ice I stepped down. Then everything went black because either Charlie Conacher or Day threw a mittful of chimney soot in my face. They showed no respect for royalty at all. So when the lights came up I stood there looking like a king all right, except that my face was pitch black. It took me two or three days of hard scrubbing to get the darn stuff off.

But it turned out to be a fantastic night and I have wonderful memories of it. They gave me a grandfather's clock which still keeps real good time. And a silver tea service for my wife. I think I was the first Leaf player ever to be given a "night," and the prime movers behind the salute were Mr. Smythe and Mr. Selke. It was one of the greatest things that ever happened to me in sports.

Anyway, I wore my green uniform for the first period of the game that followed. After the first period, Lester Patrick, the Ranger coach, told me I'd better change back to a blue shirt because the green sweater with the shamrock on back was confusing to the other players.

I didn't play well that night. I was just too emotional after all that had happened. I was too wrought up to even make a proper speech when they threw a microphone in front of me. I was absolutely tongue-tied, and that's quite an admission for an Irish gabber like me.

When I look back over the years to that St. Patrick's Day in 1934, to that "night" of mine and all the nights of hockey that went before it and came after it, I realize it's the friends I've made that count. After all, having a lot of good friends and making sure you get along with people is what life is all about, isn't it?

––––––––––

King Clancy sparked the Leafs to a Stanley Cup triumph in 1932. He retired during the 1936–37 season and coached the Montreal Maroons the following season. Then he turned to refereeing and became one of the most respected officials in the game. He coached the Leafs from 1950 to 1953 and served the club after that as assistant general manager and "vice-president in charge of nothing" — to borrow his own job description.

Clancy Decides to Get Even

FORMER NHLer "Peanuts" O'Flaherty tells this story about Leaf Hall-of-Famer King Clancy:

> King told me this story himself so it must be true. He was playing for Toronto back in '34, when he crossed centre ice and ran smack into big Art Somers. It was a vicious check and Clancy crashed to the ice and was badly hurt.

Clancy once told writer Trent Frayne that Somers gave him a butt-end in the face, splitting his tongue and knocking out four teeth. What bothered Clancy more than anything was that the gum he was chewing got stuck in his teeth.

> Clancy went home to Ottawa in the off-season and brought a pair of elbow pads with him. Over the summer he sliced open the pads, removed some of the padding, and filled the pads with buckshot pellets.
>
> In those days we wore our elbow pads on the outside of our sweaters. When a new season got underway, in the first game between the Rangers and the Leafs, Clancy caught Somers skating with his head down. He threw an elbow that broke Somers's jaw in about 14 places. Somers was hospitalized and the next day his doctors said there were "serious complications." The Ranger star was on the "danger list" for several days and played in only seven games that season. Clancy had popped him a lot harder than he intended to, but then they played the game a little rougher in those days.

The Tackweight Kid
Pulls a Frank Merriwell

T HE Tackweight Kid was another moniker for the Leafs' Bob Gracie, a North Bay native who weighed in at 155 pounds when he joined the club in 1931 and scored four goals in eight games. In 1931–32 he collected 13 goals in the 48-game schedule and snared three more goals in seven playoff matches. It was his finest NHL season. He stayed another season with the Leafs, then drifted around the league for the rest of the decade, performing with the Bruins, the Americans, the Maroons, the Canadiens, and the Blackhawks.

This story is about his biggest goal, one of three playoff goals he scored in the spring of 1932, one of only four playoff goals he scored in his career. Lou Marsh, sports editor of the *Toronto Star* in that era, tabbed Gracie "the Tackweight Kid" after a semifinal game at Maple Leaf Gardens between the Leafs and the Montreal Maroons. On April 4, 1932, Marsh wrote:

> Fidgeting on the players' bench up at the Big House of Hockey on Saturday night — the score a 2–2 tie on the game and a 3–3 tie on the semi final Stanley Cup round — five minutes of overtime gone — a pale-faced tackweight Maple Leaf rookie, lightest man on the team, hitched over to silver-haired Dick Irvin, the coach of the Leafs, and said, "Gee, I feel like I'm gonna score the winning goal for you. Let me out there."
>
> Ten seconds later there was a stop in the play. Irvin, the Old Fox of Regina, flagged his flashy Kid Line to the bench and tumbled his Pepper Line overboard. The last man of the Pepper Line out was the Tackweight Kid, this pale-faced rookie.
>
> "Go get your Stanley Cup goal, kid," said coach Irvin.

Half a minute later, the pasty-faced kid raced down to the Maroons' blue line and as he rode across the mark whipped a drive that landed in the nets behind "Flat" Walsh.

The red light twinkled.

Fifteen thousand nerve-wracked fans tore loose a yell that died to a concerted sort of snarling rage as referee Mike Rodden's whistle cut a shrill path through the vocal maelstrom.

Andy Blair's steel shod brogans were over the line before the puck by inches and Mike had called a real close one against his hometown team. "Robbed!" ten thousand screamed in a rage-smeared crescendo. Wow! How they howled and hooted and squawled!

The crowd knew Mike was right — but they wanted that goal — such a measly technicality. Wanted it whether Mike was right or wrong — wanted it because it would have relieved nerves as tight as fiddle strings, and raw with tension — nerves that gnawed like a thousand toothaches.

But if Mike had ever given it to them they would have despised him forever! Mike was right and they knew it!

They howled and hurled vicious taunts and bloody threats just because they were half mad from the strain of the most nerve-wracking game that has been played here this season. But Rodden called the infraction of the so and so blue line rule and the rookie did not get his Stanley Cup goal.

At least not then.

"This isn't my spot," he wailed to Irvin as he came off with the rest of his line.

"You'll get it yet," declared the foxy Irvin for he knew his psychology.

Ten minutes later Irvin shot out the Pepper Line again. When they were lining up, the Tackweight Kid leaned over the fence to Bill Graham, the official scorekeeper and statistician, and yelled, "Bill, you can chalk me down for the winning goal right now."

"Show me," said Silent Bill.

Ten seconds later he had it. Ten seconds later, Andy Blair, the Manitoba Mystery Man, snared the battered slice of gutta percha at mid-ice and raced down the right boards. The Tackweight Kid went with him — but away across the ice on the opposite wing. At the blue line Blair whipped a long pass over.

The Tackweight Kid grabbed it on the blue line — a perfect pass and a perfect pickup. He was coming like a flash — the Howie Morenz of his team. Halfway in to the goal, he swung and rifled one at "Flat" Walsh from an angle.

Walsh kicked at the black smudge that was the flying puck — caught it on his pads halfway between his knee and his ankle. The puck dropped twisting, struck on a corner — and landed in the net!

There was an instant's silence — tense yet vibrant — one, two, three seconds. A half sob, half wail arose from the packed tiers.

Then the red light blinked!

And bedlam broke loose!

Dozens of hats flew out upon the ice . . . programs too . . . everybody sprang to his or her feet . . . or his or her neighbour's feet . . . shouts . . . stamps . . . screams . . . whistles . . . hats were broken and shoulders slapped.

Harold Cotton did a weird war dance in mid-ice. He threw his gloves and his stick high in the air.

A woman fainted.

The Tackweight Kid — Bob Gracie — had made good. He was carried off the ice on the shoulders of his battered and leg-weary comrades.

The Leafs had won . . . 3–3 on the game . . . 4–3 on the round.

The Leafs rode into the Stanley Cup finals on the shoulders of the Tackweight Kid. Back in November the Tackweight Kid was all but "sold down the river!"

Maybe that shot won the Stanley Cup. Who can tell?

It made Bob Gracie of North Bay, Kirkland Lake and Toronto, king for a night!

The Leafs went on to win the Stanley Cup that season, beating the Rangers in three straight games, 6–4, 6–2, and 6–4. Five seasons later, Bob Gracie scored his fourth and final playoff goal — for the Montreal Maroons in a 4–1 victory over Boston.

An In-Depth Look
at the Alfie Moore Caper

D OES the name Alfie Moore still ring a hockey bell? Let me give you the basics of his 60-minute moment of hockey glory, and then we'll add some little-known facts about the incident.

In the spring of 1938, the lowly Chicago Blackhawks, winners of only 14 games all season and guided by former baseball umpire and NHL referee Bill Stewart, caught fire in the playoffs. After ousting the Montreal Canadiens and the New York Rangers, the Hawks found themselves in the finals against Toronto.

There was much gloom in the Chicago camp prior to game one at Maple Leaf Gardens. Netminder Mike Karakas, an American-born player from Aurora, Minnesota, could not suit up because of a broken toe. The Hawks were in a pickle because their spare goaltender was playing in Wichita, Kansas, hundreds of miles away.

Bill Tobin, assistant to Chicago owner Major Fred McLaughlin, contacted NHL president Frank Calder and requested permission to use Dave Kerr, the New York Rangers' netminder and a Toronto native, as a replacement for Karakas. Calder said Kerr could play providing the Leafs and the Rangers consented to the proposal.

Tobin received permission from New York but Leaf owner Conn Smythe wasn't so quick to go along. Kerr was a damn fine goalie and Smythe could picture him leading the Hawks to the Stanley Cup. "Why not use Alfie Moore, a minor league netminder?" asked Smythe. "He's a good old Toronto boy and he's available."

Moore was a former Leaf farmhand who'd been toiling for years in the minor leagues. After much discussion, Smythe and Tobin agreed to meet again at the Gardens one hour before game time. By then perhaps Karakas's swollen foot might be encased in a skate and the Hawks' goaltending problem would evaporate.

The second session involved Smythe, his second in command, Frank Selke, Bill Tobin, and his manager-coach, Bill Stewart, along with president Calder. The medical report on Karakas was not good. He would not be able to play. By then Calder had decided to deny Chicago's request to use Kerr.

Frank Selke, meanwhile, had arranged for Alfie Moore to come to the Gardens, and he was sipping coffee in a nearby room. Tobin exploded when he learned of this and accused Selke and Smythe of forcing him to use a player who was not only inferior but not even sober. Earlier in the day, while drinking beer at an east-end tavern, Moore had purchased a pair of tickets for the game from his friends on the Chicago team. Selke and Smythe resented Tobin's accusation that they'd tried to pull a fast one and hot words were exchanged.

The late Andy Lytle, sports editor of the *Toronto Star*, was on the scene that night tracking developments and wrote the following:

> I was leaning against a Garden wall opposite the press room talking to Frank Selke. It was a few minutes to game time and the crowd was filling in rapidly. Smythe joined us and began talking about the developments which had culminated in Alfie Moore taking Mike Karakas' place in the Hawk nets when Bill Tobin came up. Soon he and Smythe were in heated debate.
>
> Tobin turned away when Smythe very emphatically informed him what he thought of him. As he left, Bill Stewart came up and said to Selke: "Frank, I didn't think you would turn out to be a liar."
>
> "Nobody can call Selke a liar in my presence," exploded

Smythe. "You've been threatening to lick the whole league for two years now. Let's see what you've got."

As he was speaking, Smythe stepped in and swung. Stewart sprang at him. In a moment they were struggling fiercely. Half a dozen peacemakers barged right in. Soon the combatants were separated, Smythe being held by three or four willing hands and Stewart shoved towards the ice by Harold Cotton, King Clancy and Joe Primeau. They were trying to hold the irate Chicagoan but it was a difficult task.

Stewart was fuming and struggling like a man gone mad. Meantime, Smythe was shaking off the peacemakers, telling one or two of them where to go and striving to get at Stewart. Stewart got back to his dressing room but not before he and Cotton had threatened to tear each other apart. Smythe was induced to go into the Leafs' room.

At the end of the second period, I was talking with Karakas and Stewart at the Hawks' dressing room door when Cotton hove into Bill's view. At once the two opened verbal fire at one another like two excited macaws. Cotton was telling Bill what he would do to him and Bill was throwing each defiance right back at Baldy. Suddenly Cotton moved in. Bill shoved us aside as he sprang to battle. Next second they were into it, hell for leather. This too was a brief skirmish, with Cotton landing some telling punches before they were separated. Cotton was wild with rage after Stewart referred to him as a particularly clinging type of domesticated insect.

A policeman shoved Stewart into his room. Cotton was shoved into the press room. Cotton was still breathing defiances. Suddenly he looked up and laughed: "You know," he said, "that's the first manager I ever licked. It felt swell."

While all this was going on, Tobin, club mouthpiece for Major McLaughlin and a busy politician at all times, raced around the rink and informed Frank Calder he'd better come over and see Bill Stewart because "he is being cut to ribbons by wild Toronto men" or words to that alarming effect.

Calder went to the room where he found Stewart raving and swearing he would kill Cotton. Calder is understood to have examined Stewart for marks of combat and to have found one or two slight scratches. Calder tried to find out from Stewart what had taken place but by this time Stewart was incoherent.

As it turned out, Moore took his place in goal and turned out to be the hero of the game, Chicago winning 3–1. He was called on to make several brilliant saves and put his thumb to his nose when he left, an indication of how he felt about Smythe and the Leafs. He departed a happy man. After all, he had been with so many bad teams in the minors it was only recently he found out that hockey was a game played with only one puck.

It turned out to be Moore's most memorable day in hockey. In the afternoon he'd been sitting quietly having a beer when a man showed up and said, "Alfie, they want you to play goal for Chicago tonight. Get your gear!"

"I'll get my gear," he replied nonchalantly, "as soon as I finish this quart."

Alfie's confidence was hardly bolstered by his younger brother Laurie, who once was a goalie but gave it up. When he heard that Alfie would be in goal, Laurie ran outside the bar and threw up.

Another brother, Freddy, listened to the game on the radio that night. Freddy, crippled since he was kicked in the head during a football game seven years earlier, cheered Alfie's every move during the contest.

"You know, I was pretty hot before the game," Alfie told reporters after his once-in-a-lifetime performance. "I felt I was getting pushed around. At six o'clock I was sitting there not knowing whether I'd play or not. I guess all that arguing got to me. And I was still hot after the game. But I was hot during the game and that's what really counts."

The second game was played two nights later. By then the Hawks had located spare goaltender Paul Goodman, a player

Stewart had never met, and the newcomer played in goal when Moore was ruled ineligible. Goodman was bombed for five goals and the Leafs won the game easily by a 5–1 score. But Chicago, with Karakas back in harness, roared back on home ice and won two straight games and the Stanley Cup.

The Night Clancy Suckered Shore

THERE it was on the front page of the Toronto *Globe*:

Sensational Comeback as Leafs Win Playoff. Bang in Six Goals in One Period — Conacher Gets Three.

The date was March 26, 1936, the day of the second game of a torrid playoff series between the Leafs and the Boston Bruins. It was a two-game, total-goals-to-count affair in those days and the Leafs had dropped the opener in Boston by a 3–0 score. Their chances of advancing to the next round against the Americans appeared to be hopeless. And almost impossible when the Bruins scored early in the second game to open up a 4–0 margin.

But when the game was over, Don Cowie, a young reporter bursting with excitement, tapped out the following for the morning edition:

Toronto 8; Boston 3. Wow!! What a game!! They said it was impossible, folks. But the impossible happened. We've never seen a game like that one. And probably will never see another.

That is just a way of recording the most sensational comeback in playoff hockey history. Maple Leafs stamped themselves as one of the greatest "fighting"

hockey machines of all time as they upset the dope sheet completely at Maple Leaf Gardens by outfighting the Boston Bruins 8–3, took the Stanley Cup playoff round 8–6, and qualified to face the New York Americans in the semifinal series.

A capacity crowd went mad as the Leafs, "rank outsiders," scored the most stunning upset in many hockey moons. The turning point in the game came in the second period when Bruin ace Eddie Shore took a minor penalty. While he was off, Clancy and Conacher scored for the Leafs. Another blazing series of Leaf raids culminated when Red Horner, who installed himself in the goal crease so long he could have drawn a parking ticket, rapped the third goal home.

The Bruins hotly berated referee Cleghorn for allowing that goal. Shore in particular was incensed. That's when King Clancy pulled a cute little trick. He sidled over to Shore and commiserated with him. "That was a rotten call, Eddie, just a lousy decision. I don't blame you for being sore." A fuming Shore, fire in his eye, grabbed the loose puck and fired it at Cleghorn, and the hard rubber disc stung the official. Caught in the act, Shore drew a 10-minute misconduct while Clancy tried to hide his smirk.

With Shore off for half the period, the Leafs rolled to the attack and punched home three more quick goals, two with the man advantage. They walloped the staggering Bruins 8–3 and captured the series 8–6.

They went on to eliminate the New York Americans in the follow-up series but were defeated in the Stanley Cup finals by the Detroit Red Wings.

Eddie Shore was named the league's MVP four times and was voted to the All-Star team seven times. He had his nose broken 14 times and his jaw fractured five times. He lost most of his teeth and accumulated an estimated 970 stitches in his tough hide.

THE FORTIES

Hockey's Most Incredible Comeback

OLDTIME Leaf fans will never forget the Stanley Cup final series in 1942. It matched the Leafs, coached by Hap Day, versus Jack Adams's Detroit Red Wings. There's never been a series quite like it.

For starters, the Leafs were fortunate to be in the finals. In the first round of the playoffs against New York, the NHL's top team, it took a winning goal by Nick Metz with seven seconds left to play in the deciding game to propel the Leafs into the final series.

Playing for the Stanley Cup against the Red Wings, the Leafs were odds-on favourites. Hadn't they finished the regular season with eight more wins and 15 more points than the Wings? But the Leafs stumbled through the first two games on home ice and lost them both. Then they dropped the third game back in Detroit. Leaf fans were frustrated and furious. Abuse fell like shrapnel and the Toronto sportswriters were merciless in their criticism of the coach and the players. Fans sneered at Day's name and said he was no coach. Andy Lytle of the *Toronto Star* wrote, "Except for the gate receipts and the records, there is little apparent use in prolonging this series."

Hap Day told the Toronto directors that Detroit's style had his team buffaloed. It marked the first time a team had shot the puck into the Leaf zone and flooded in after it. In those days there was no centre-ice red line. The Wings simply worked the puck over their blue line and fired it into the Toronto zone. Day told the directors that defenceman Bucko McDonald was worn out and that Gordon Drillon's style wasn't suited to the unorthodox shoot-and-skate style of the Red Wings.

"Are there any other players available?" he was asked.

"Well, yes, there's Ernie Dickens and Don Metz," he replied. "They're green but I'll work them in and drop McDonald and Drillon. We'll also change our style and play the same way the Red Wings are playing. Maybe we can beat them at their own game."

Don Metz was an unlikely replacement for Drillon, the team's leading scorer. Metz had scored just two goals all season, while Drillon finished eighth in the NHL scoring race with 23 goals and 41 points. Ernie Dickens was another two-goal man, a lad who'd played only 10 NHL games in his life.

In game four on Detroit ice, Nick Metz, brother of Don, got the winner in a 4–3 victory and the Red Wings put the champagne back in the cooler. Their coach and manager, Jack Adams, also required some cooling down. He was suspended for the rest of the series after he leaped on the ice after the game and attacked referee Mel Harwood, who was badly mauled in a free-for-all that was triggered by Eddie Wares and Don Grosso of the Wings.

In game five Don Metz scored a hat trick, Syl Apps picked up a pair of goals, and the Leafs romped to a 9–3 triumph. Andy Lytle wrote, "This series gets curiouser and curiouser. Only Alice in Wonderland would believe it from beginning to end."

.It was back to Detroit for game six, where Turk Broda had a hot night and blanked the Red Wings 3–0. In game seven the fans almost broke down the doors at Maple Leaf Gardens in their frantic efforts to see the game. A record crowd of almost 17,000 witnessed the culmination of the most incredible comeback in playoff history, ending when the Leafs' Sweeney Schriner scored two third-period goals and Pete Langelle added a bit of insurance in a 3–1 Toronto triumph. Hap Day and his weary men, blistered for their incompetence a few days earlier, were now the toast of the nation. Day had captured his first Stanley Cup as Maple Leaf coach. Many more would follow.

Bob Davidson, who would spend 44 years in the Toronto organization as a player and scout, played on the Leafs' Cup-winning team in 1942. He says there was some real motivation for winning.

After trailing Detroit 3–0 in the series, we had no idea we were about to make an astonishing comeback with four straight wins. Who would have believed that would happen? Aside from some player changes, two things happened to get us in a winning mood before that fourth game in Detroit. First, Jack Adams, the Detroit manager, went on radio and said his team would wrap it up in the four games. He sounded pretty cocky and it made us mad. Then Hap Day, our coach, read us a letter from a little girl in Toronto who said she'd be ashamed to go to school the next day if we lost four straight games in the finals. That inspired us to do our best. Even so, we fell behind 2–0 in the second period. Then I scored a goal that got us going and we won 4–3. We just took off after that and wouldn't be beaten. After we captured the Stanley Cup, Syl Apps and I went to visit the little girl who'd written the letter and told her how much she'd helped us.

Arrested in Boston

H ERE'S another tale from my collection of endless Clancy anecdotes. Before his death in 1986, he told me about a night in Beantown that had him chewing his fingernails.

Linesman George Hayes and I had an experience in Boston one time that all but scared me to death. My playing career was long over by then and I had turned to refereein' for a living. Musta bin sometime in the '40s when this incident happened. Hayes and I were entering our hotel when the manager came running over. "Mr. Clancy," he said, "there's a detective waiting for you and he's got a warrant for your arrest. And there's one for you too, Mr. Hayes."

I was shocked. "What's it for?" I asked. "What's this all about?"

"Did you get involved in an altercation with a fan after the game last night?"

"Oh, that," I said. "But that was nothin'."

It was true that one of those hot-headed Bruin fans had come round to the referee's room to sound off about the officiating. He wanted to tell referee George Gravelle (I had been a linesman in the game that night) just what he thought of him. Just for fun, I opened the door and pushed this guy into the room. The first guy he met in there was big George Hayes, who was taking off his skates.

"Who's this?" said Hayes.

"This is the fellow who wants to lick George Gravelle," I said, nudging the guy a little closer to Hayes.

"Well, he's got to lick me first," Hayes replied. Then he got up and grabbed the fan by the shirt and gave him a little toss across the room. Then he turned him around, booted him in the ass, and threw him out of the dressing room.

And now, a few hours later, here we were under arrest and on our way to court. The press got wind of it and flashbulbs are popping outside the courtroom. You'd think Hayes and Clancy were names from the Ten Most Wanted List.

The court clerk came over and asked me my name and when and where I was born. Then he asked me if I'd ever been in trouble with the law. I said, "No sir, not me. I have never been in court in my life. This is my first time and I want you to know I feel terrible about it."

Then it was Hayes's turn. When he asked George if he'd ever been in trouble before, he replied, "Oh, sure, lots of times. Back home, I was up for assault and battery."

I nearly died when he said that. Assault and battery was the charge they were laying against us.

80

We both testified to what happened at the game and when the fan spoke he painted us out to be a couple of thugs who beat him up without any reason for it. Throughout the hearing Hayes sat there calmly while I was shaking like a leaf and wondering what the inside of a Boston jail looked like and whether I'd lose my job. In the end the judge let us go for lack of evidence but not before he said he doubted the veracity of some of my remarks. Then he said to Hayes, "Mr. Hayes, I want to congratulate you on your testimony. You left a good impression here today."

Don't think I wasn't put out about that! I hadn't done anything to be brought into court in the first place. Sure I pushed the guy into the dressing room, but I wasn't the one who picked him up and tossed him around or booted him in the ass.

Years later, Lester Patrick of the Rangers talked to me about that incident. He said, "King, that was a ticklish situation. I heard that two policemen on duty that night told the judge they didn't see very much. They didn't see you push the guy into the room and they didn't see anyone push him out. They said they saw him fall on his face in the corridor. And that was about it. You know, King, I can't help but think those two cops must have been Irishmen."

I laughed and said, "Lester, what the hell do you think the judge was — a Hungarian?"

George Hayes was one of the strongest and toughest officials ever to work the lines in the NHL. He became the first official to work in more than 1,000 games, ending his 19-year career with 1,544 regular-season games. He officiated in 149 playoff games and 11 All-Star games. He was inducted (posthumously) into the Hockey Hall of Fame in 1988.

Gaye Stewart, Jimmy Orlando in Battle Royal

O N November 7, 1942, at Maple Leaf Gardens, Gaye Stewart of the Leafs, the youngster who beat out Rocket Richard, Glen Harmon, and others for the rookie award in the previous season, was barrelling down the boards in a game against Detroit. The Wings' tough defenceman Jimmy Orlando lined him up and dumped him in a heap of white and blue in the corner. Stewart scrambled up and nailed Orlando with a slash to the body, a loss of temper that earned him a two-minute respite in the penalty box, thanks to the keen eyes of referee King Clancy.

In the words of Orlando:

> Stewart entered the box like an enraged bull. The guy was so mad he couldn't sit down and he kept hollerin' at me all through the next shift. When I hollered somethin' back, that did it! He leaped out of the box even though he still had a minute to serve and comes at me while the play is going the other way. I see him coming, drop my gloves and nail him a good one. He hit the deck and Clancy don't see this one 'cause he's way up the ice. Stewart leaps up and smashes me with his stick right across the skull — a vicious two-hander. His stick cut me for 23 stitches and I don't know whether I'm on the ice or knocking at St. Peter's door. I'm not too clear on what happened after that but I sure as hell didn't get to hit him with my stick, as hard as I might have tried. Don't believe me? Well, even back then they had films of the games and as Casey Stengel used to say, "you could look it up."

It took all three officials to restrain Orlando before he was finally taken to the Red Wing dressing room where the loose ends of his scalp were stitched together. Clancy gave both players match penalties and referred the incident to NHL president Frank Calder for further discipline. The combatants were subsequently fined $100 each. Orlando was suspended from playing any games in Toronto for the rest of the season and Stewart was barred from playing in Detroit. These suspensions were later rescinded.

Billy Taylor:
Suspended for Life

BILLY Taylor was destined to become a Leaf star from the age of 12. When the Gardens opened in 1931–32, he was the team mascot. The popular neophyte demonstrated his skating ability between periods, and when the Leafs won the Stanley Cup in 1932, Taylor had a front-row seat — right on the team bench.

He grew up to be a fast and clever centreman, one of the best stickhandlers in the game. Early on he learned to carry the puck with his head up because he didn't have the size to shake off heavy checks. When he broke in with the Leafs in 1939, he weighed a mere 140 pounds and stood five foot eight. But my, how he could fly! And he could fight, too. In 1947, by then a Red Wing, he was involved in a classic punchout with Leaf rookie Howie Meeker. They hammered each other on the ice and then in the penalty box. Before it was over, all three game officials, 12 policemen, several ushers, and a number of fans invaded the penalty box. Finally, Taylor and Meeker were banished from the game. In the spring of 1942, when the Leafs fell behind the Red Wings 3–0 in the Stanley Cup finals, Taylor was the only Leaf to predict the miraculous comeback that followed: four straight victories and a taste of champagne from the Cup.

The following season, Taylor scored 60 points in 50 games, an outstanding achievement for the era. He left hockey for two years to serve overseas, and when he returned in 1945–46 he collected 23 goals in 48 games, his career high. Then, despite the fancy statistics, came the shock of a trade to Detroit — for left winger Harry Watson.

"I was traded because I made a big mistake," Taylor told sportswriter Rick Boulton several years later. "I stupidly asked for a raise. Mr. Smythe said he wasn't going to give me one penny more and packed me off to Detroit for big Harry Watson. That decision hurt me deeply because I'd been with the Leaf organization all my life."

In Detroit he teamed up with rookie Gordie Howe as a line-mate, and during a 10–6 rout of Chicago one night, he established a scoring record with seven assists. Taylor liked to remind people that his seven-assist game took place on the road — at the Chicago Stadium. "If you got seven assists in a game in those days, away from home, you knew you'd earned every one. The home team employed scorers who handed out lots of assists on the home team's goals but were often stingy with the credit when the opposing team scored. We beat Chicago 10–6 that night and three of my assists led to Roy Conacher's hat trick." The only other NHLer to collect seven assists in a game is Wayne Gretzky. He did it three times, twice on Edmonton ice and once in Chicago.

"I had a great year with the Wings in '46–47 until I got sick near the end," Taylor recalled. "I led the team in scoring and finished third in league scoring behind Max Bentley and Maurice Richard. Now I felt sure I deserved a raise over the $9,000 I was earning. But when I asked Jack Adams for a hike in salary he said he couldn't do it because I'd taken sick. What's more he said he would have to cut my salary by a thousand bucks because I might be sick again the following season. I was so mad I told him I was going home. The next day I went out and bought a paper and read that I'd been traded to Boston. You didn't pop off to the bosses in those days."

Leaf coach Hap Day was one hockey man Taylor admired. Day slipped him a $2,000 bonus in 1943, when Conn Smythe was busy leading a battalion overseas and Day was serving as acting manager of the Leafs in Smythe's absence. "He was a great coach," recalled Taylor. "One of the smartest coaches I ever saw. He and Smythe both liked to give pep talks. Smythe blistered me one night between periods. 'Taylor, you haven't even worked up a sweat!' he bellowed. From then on when I came in after each period, I splashed water on my head and face. One night Smythe blistered everybody else but when he looked at me he saw how wet I was and he said, 'Taylor, you're the only one who's working hard out there.'"

Taylor's exceptional career came to a sudden end in 1947. In a shocking pronouncement, NHL President Clarence Campbell suspended Taylor, by then a New York Ranger, and Don Gallinger of the Boston Bruins, for life after declaring he had proof they'd been associating with gamblers and wagering on NHL games. There was little evidence to indicate that the players bet against their own teams and both men claimed they never did. But Gallinger, years later, revealed that he and Taylor, while playing for Boston, had conspired to do just that. On one occasion, Gallinger confessed to author Dick Beddoes, they each bet $1,500 (at 2–1 odds) against the Bruins to win in Chicago. Then Gallinger helped set up the go-ahead goal for Boston, saying to himself, "You dummy, you've just blown three grand." Gallinger made seven or eight bets on games and never won one of them. He not only lost his wagers, but in exile he lost his marriage, his business, and his daughter to bone cancer, and he spent some time in a mental institution.

Taylor never denied his role in the gambling scandal, never asked for reinstatement, and remained an outcast from hockey for almost a quarter of a century. Reinstated without fanfare in 1970, he returned to the game as a scout. For years, on the first Friday in May, he was a welcome guest at our annual NHL Old-timers reunion in Markham, Ontario, where he mixed well with the other ex-pros. Nobody ever inquired about his scandalous past. Perhaps they felt, "There but for the grace of God . . ." Billy Taylor died of a heart attack in June 1990.

It's ironic that Clarence Campbell, 18 months into his stint as NHL president, would ban Taylor and Gallinger for life, in light of the sentence handed Babe Pratt of the Leafs a few months earlier — in 1946. Pratt was suspended for a little more than two weeks after he admitted he bet on games involving the Leafs. Frank Calder, Campbell's predecessor, appealed to the league governors on Pratt's behalf, pointing out Babe's honesty in offering a prompt confession. Pratt was quickly reinstated and in time would become an honoured member of the Hockey Hall of Fame. Taylor and Gallinger were not so fortunate. Taylor's words, oft-repeated, aptly described their predicament: "We've paid and paid and paid."

––––––––––

It's also ironic that Campbell, who talked of the "stigma and humiliation" and his "feelings of indignation" that accompanied the suspensions of Taylor and Gallinger, a man who championed the integrity of the league, should be found guilty in 1980 of conspiracy to give Louis Giguere, a Quebec senator, $95,000 in exchange for an extension on the lease of the duty-free Sky Shops at Montreal's Dorval Airport. Campbell served five hours in jail and was fined $25,000. Some might say his indiscretions surpassed those of the two young players he turfed out of hockey.

Bodnar's Records Still Stand

IT happened a long time ago, on the night of October 30, 1943. The Leafs were playing the New York Rangers on the opening night of the new season and rookie Gus Bodnar, a Fort William, Ontario, native, was sent out to take the opening face-off. He not only won the draw but he stepped around his opposing centre, waltzed in on goal, and scored! The Sportimer overhead showed just 15 seconds had elapsed. Bodnar's fast work gave him much-needed confidence and he enjoyed a splendid rookie season, compiling 22 goals and 40 assists for 62 points, statistics impressive enough to capture the Calder Trophy as the NHL's top rookie.

Bodnar's penchant for fast scoring wasn't confined to his freshman season. On March 13, 1952, while playing for Chicago against New York, he set up three goals by linemate Bill Mosienko — in a record time of 21 seconds. Both of Bodnar's marks — fastest goal by a rookie from the start of a game and fastest three assists — still stand. Bodnar played four seasons with Toronto and seven more with Chicago. He wound up his career with a season in Boston. While most players improve on their freshman scoring stats as they gain experience, Bodnar was never able to match or surpass his rookie season totals, 22 goals and 62 points.

Trade Coup a Costly One for Selke

I N 1943 the Leafs signed a promising defenceman named Frank Eddolls to a contract. But Eddolls joined the RCAF and soon began playing some hockey for an air force team in and around Montreal. There he caught the eye of Canadiens' coach Dick Irvin.

Irvin called Frank Selke in Toronto and asked if Eddolls was available. And if so, what would the Leafs want in return?

"You've got a teenager in Port Colborne who shows some promise," replied Selke. "Name's Ted Kennedy. We might take a chance on him if you want Eddolls." Selke didn't tell Irvin that Kennedy's coach, former NHL star Nels Stewart, had been imploring Selke to make a deal for Kennedy if at all possible.

the Cup hopes of the blue and white underdogs. The latter proved to be the case in game five as the Leafs suffered a 10–3 trouncing. Rocket Richard was a formidable force, collecting four of the Montreal goals.

Back in Toronto in game six, goalie Frank McCool, who drank from a bottle of milk between periods to calm his inflamed ulcers, shrugged off Richard's goal grab and came through with a dazzling performance. Veteran Sweeney Schriner made the plays that led to a 3–2 Leaf victory, a stunning upset, and a berth in the finals.

McCool was brilliant again in the opener against Detroit and skated off with a 1–0 shutout. In game two he did it again, blanking the Red Wing shooters as the Leafs won 2–0. It was more McCool magic in game three. He handled 29 shots and was flawless again. Three games, three shutouts! Leaf fans were thrilled, and the Red Wings could only shake their heads in disbelief.

Outspoken Red Wing manager Jack Adams was disgusted with the clutch-and-grab tactics of the Leafs and blamed Hap Day. He snarled, "Day came in here and stunk out the joint. I guess this is the spring of the big stink."

McCool's remarkable streak came to an end midway through the first period in game four when Flash Hollett scored for Detroit. Leaf captain Ted Kennedy almost won the game single-handedly with a hat trick, but the Wings scored three times in the third period and won the game 5–3.

McCool had his sights set on a fourth shutout in game five and held the Wings off the scoresheet until well into the third period. But Harry Lumley in the Detroit goal matched him save for save. Then Flash Hollet beat McCool, and Joe Carveth scored an insurance marker with time running out. Detroit won 2–0.

Shutout goaltending was the story again in game six with McCool and Lumley keeping their nets free of pucks for three periods of play. In overtime Eddie Bruneteau, a fringe player for Detroit, beat McCool to force a seventh and deciding game back in Detroit.

"Revenge for 1942" was now the Red Wing rallying cry. How the Detroit fans wanted to stick it to the Leafs and remind them that they too were capable of climbing back from a three-game deficit. They confidently predicted that the stigma of the 1942 humiliation would soon be erased.

The Detroit Olympia was jammed full for game seven. Toronto's Mel Hill scored the first goal, and the 1–0 lead held up until the third period when Murray Armstrong slipped through the Toronto defence to tie the score. But four minutes later big Babe Pratt, holder of the Hart Trophy in the previous season, finished off a rush by scoring a power-play goal against Lumley, and the Leafs hung on to win 2–1.

Day had used only 11 players in each playoff game except the final one. Then he finally threw out his third line — the Metz brothers and Art Jackson.

There was no victory parade around the Olympia with the Stanley Cup held aloft, no postgame champagne party for the new champions. The Leafs threw off their uniforms and rushed to catch the train to Toronto. And when they arrived back at Union Station at daybreak the next morning, there were only a handful of friends and relatives to meet them and offer congratulations.

Rebuilding the Club

A FTER winning the Stanley Cup in 1945, and after promising their fans they'd "do it again in '46," the Leafs stumbled badly the following season. They finished in fifth place and missed the playoffs.

Conn Smythe was irate and placed most of the blame for the disaster on Frank Selke, who promptly resigned and joined the Montreal Canadiens as managing director.

Smythe decided it was time for sweeping changes. He would rebuild his club. Some of the Leaf veterans said they'd had enough and retired, among them Sweeney Schriner, Lorne Carr, and Bob Davidson. Babe Pratt, suspended for a few days during the season for wagering on hockey games, was sold to Boston. Billy Taylor, who would later be suspended for life for wagering on games, went to Detroit in a trade for big Harry Watson, a future Hall-of-Famer.

Six rookies were brought in and four were defencemen. Garth Boesch, Jim Thompson, Bill Barilko, and Gus Mortson became overnight favourites on the Leaf blue line. Up front, Howie Meeker, fully recovered from shrapnel wounds suffered during the war, set his sights on the Calder Trophy as Rookie-of-the-Year and won it with 27 goals and 45 points, totals he would never reach again. Vic Lynn was acquired from the Canadiens and won a spot.

Experts predicted a lengthy struggle until the inexperienced newcomers adjusted to the fast pace of NHL play. But the blend of youth and experience (holdovers were Broda, Apps, Kennedy, Stanowski, the Metz brothers, Ezinicki, and Stewart) paid off handsomely and quickly. The Leafs took a leap in the standings, challenged Montreal for first place, and captured the Stanley Cup in the spring of '47 (see page 95). They won it again in '48, after completing a monster deal with Chicago to land Max Bentley. The Leafs pounded Detroit in the finals, winning four straight and holding the powerful Production Line of Howe, Abel, and Lindsay to a single goal. In '49 it was more of the same when the Leafs and the Red Wings clashed in the finals. Goaltender Turk Broda stymied the Production Line again, after the threesome had pumped 12 of 17 Detroit goals past Montreal in a semifinal series. Broda allowed just five goals in four games, Sid Smith collected a hat trick in game two, and Toronto swept the Red Wings aside in four matches. The triumph, the Leafs' second four-game sweep in two seasons, made them the first NHL team to roll to three straight Stanley Cups.

Yes indeed, Smythe had completed a masterful rebuilding job.

———

I worked with Howie Meeker for many years on *Hockey Night in Canada* and was surprised the first time I heard him say, "I was a dumb hockey player who learned how to pass and skate after my career was over — at age 35. I taught myself how to pass properly after I was finished in the NHL. No one had ever shown me. As for skating, Teeder Kennedy was a marvellous player who could do everything but skate well. Today I could show him how to improve his skating but I couldn't help him when I played with him. I didn't know enough then." Howie pondered the basics of the game, questioning everything from how to fit skates on young feet to how to finish a check. Thousands of players have benefitted from his advice, through his books, TV shows, and his hockey schools. His contributions to the game have been enormous.

Pratt Has Big Problems

ON a cold day in January 1946, NHL president Red Dutton expelled defenceman Walter "Babe" Pratt of the Toronto Maple Leafs from the National Hockey League. Pratt was barred from further play because he persisted in gambling on the outcome of games after being warned not to do so.

Dutton said his investigations had shown, and Pratt had admitted, association with known gamblers. "What could we do with the big lug?" asked Dutton. "He's no rookie. Been in the league 11 years. He knows the league rules and laws. Mind you, I have no proof that Pratt bet against his own team. But we can't let such things as he has admitted go on in hockey."

Pratt, who had won the Hart Trophy two years earlier, told reporters, "I am innocent of any feeling of wrong-doing. I never made a bet against the Leafs in my life. I admitted to Dutton that I've made wagers. Sure I have. I've also made bets on horse races. Who hasn't?

"I also assured Dutton I would never make a wager on hockey again. Nor will I ever be seen in the company of gamblers. I want to get out of this jam and back to playing hockey. I'm a $6,000 a year guy. I can't afford not to continue at my hockey job. Where else can I make that kind of money swinging a pick and shovel?"

Dutton said, "Babe has been betting on games for a long time. And he was losing most of his bets. So the fear arose: If a player keeps on losing bets, isn't it logical to assume that, in desperation, he might bet against his own team and think more of winning the bet than winning the game?"

Noted New York sportswriter Dan Parker wrote:

> **If Babe Pratt's only offence was in betting on games (and then, never against his own club) where do the holier-than-thou race track gambling men who dominate professional hockey get off in denying him a means of livelihood by tossing him out without an open hearing?**
>
> **Remember when the NHL wasn't so holy and Butch Keeling owned a string of race horses on which all the players bet? And when an usher who had tossed out a gambler he had seen talking with a goalie was reprimanded for his act and the gambler permitted to return to the arena? That was back in 1927.**
>
> **I'm not trying to justify gambling by athletes, but if their employers bet on horse races, own racing stables and run race tracks, on what moral grounds do they base their opposition to gambling by their players?**

When W. H. A. "Bill" MacBrien, vice-president of Maple Leaf Gardens, was asked about Pratt's chances on an appeal, he replied, "They are almost nil. How can they reinstate him?"

A few days later, they did. The NHL governors unanimously pardoned Pratt, who had spent 17 days in the league's doghouse. The pardon came in the wake of an incredibly loud public outcry in favour of the player. Writers and fans pointed to the general atmosphere of gambling that pervaded hockey. Many drew attention to the wild orgies of gambling that were quite common in most of the league arenas.

Indeed, as a young boy witnessing my first hockey game at Maple Leaf Gardens, I recall staring in wonder at the large amounts of money that exchanged hands in the corridors after the contest.

Lionel Conacher, one of Canada's greatest athletes, said at the time, "It's about time hockey players quit being so stupid. How long are they going to allow officials to push them around? They should have an organization that would protect them against being crucified. Officials were bleepin' quick to assure everybody that there was no evidence that Pratt bet against his own team. On these terms, my old Montreal Maroons would have been tossed out of the league en masse."

In the *Toronto Star*, writer Andy Lytle said,

> I feel compelled to confess that I have in the past wagered sums with hockey coaches and managers still active in the NHL, on the outcome of certain matches. Would they like me to do a little stooling for them and give them the names of the offenders within their executive ranks? I'd even swear that said coaches and managers did wager against their own team and in many cases that team was the Toronto Maple Leafs.

Pratt played another season in the NHL. In 1966 he was inducted into the Hockey Hall of Fame.

Leafs Soar
When Rocket Gets Sore

DURING the 1946–47 NHL season, the Leafs and the Habs battled for the NHL's premier position, with Dick Irvin's Canadiens ultimately outpointing Hap Day's Leafs by 78 points to 72.

At season's end, the Hab's explosive winger, Rocket Richard, led all goal scorers with 45 but he seethed in frustration when Chicago's Max Bentley stole the individual scoring title — and the Art Ross Trophy — away from him by a single point. It was a trophy the Rocket coveted and one he would never capture.

The Rocket would surely have garnered a few more points during regular season play, but for an unfortunate accident to his great winger Elmer Lach. During the season, Lach was body-checked heavily by the Leafs' Don Metz and suffered a fractured skull. The incident was not forgotten when the archrivals met in the Stanley Cup finals a few weeks later.

Montreal coach Dick Irvin refused to concede that the check on Lach had been accidental, even though league officials had ruled it so.

"If we win this series with Toronto, it will prove to me the injury to Lach was deliberate," he stated angrily. "If we lose, I'll give Metz the benefit of the doubt. I believe Providence will be on our side."

Earlier, Irvin had angered Leaf fans when he journeyed to Toronto to see the junior Canadiens play. His real motive, it was reported, was to scout the Leafs in their semifinal series against Detroit. "We never scout a team we know we can beat," was Irvin's curt reply.

It certainly looked as though Providence was backing Montreal when Irvin's fired-up Habs walloped the rookie-laden Leafs 6–0 in the opening game at the Forum. After recording the shutout, goalie Bill Durnan was heard to say, "How did those guys get in the league?" Later he denied uttering those provocative words. Judging by the initial meeting, the Habs appeared capable of beating the Leafs four straight — or 12 straight.

Game two was played at the Forum two nights later. Many spectators were either repulsed or thrilled by the violence displayed. Many said they'd never seen a rougher playoff game. Early in the contest the Rocket collided with Toronto's Vic Lynn and slammed his stick across Lynn's head. Lynn was carried off the ice, leaving a trail of blood in his wake. Richard drew a major penalty.

Perhaps the Rocket spent his time in the box brooding about

his old mate Elmer Lach, for on Richard's return he went after Leaf defenceman Bill Ezinicki. Again Richard's stick crashed against a hated opponent's skull. Again a groggy Leaf player was carted off for stitching. Again a trail of blood decorated the ice.

For this second emotional outbreak Richard was given penalties totalling 20 minutes. An automatic $100 fine accompanied his misdeeds. Later he was told not to don his blades again until league president Clarence Campbell could judge his crimes. With Richard penalized for 20 long minutes, the bruised and bloodied Leafs skated off with a 4–0 victory.

The following day Campbell's sentence left Montrealers in shock. Richard was suspended for the third game of the series — the most important game of the season — and he was assessed an additional fine of $250. Montrealers were livid. Many suggested that Campbell had just handed the series to the hated Leafs.

On home ice, Toronto won game three 4–2, and afterwards Frank Selke barred reporters from the Montreal dressing room. "They've been saying things I can't believe were possible," he said angrily. Two nights later the Leafs captured game four 2–1 after 16 minutes of overtime.

Back in Montreal, fans jammed the Forum hoping to see the Rocket lead the Habs in a miraculous comeback. Hundreds of his faithful supporters had chipped in to make sure their hero did not have to pay the money he'd been fined by that unforgiving Anglo, Clarence Campbell. Richard was photographed with his hands full of bills, an amount far in excess of $250.

But the Rocket could not come up with the necessary moxie or scoring magic to answer their prayers. The Leafs won the deciding game 2–1 behind the brilliance of goalie Turk Broda, who foiled a late-game breakaway by Ken Reardon to assure the victory. One commentator called it "the wildest of all Stanley Cup series." Another wrote, "If all the hot air circulated by press and radio during the Leafs-Canadiens series had been stored, it would have created enough energy to run all the motor cars in both cities for a week."

There was no on-ice presentation following the Leafs' surprise victory. Perhaps Clarence Campbell feared an outbreak of fan violence. He told the press, "The Stanley Cup shall be presented at a time and place designated by the winners."

The week the Leafs won the Cup, hockey and homicide battled for space on the front page of the *Toronto Star*. Homicide won out when the Crown appealed Mrs. Evelyn Dick's acquittal in a sensational murder trial. Mrs. Dick had been accused of the cold-blooded murder of her husband, a Hamilton businessman. Mrs. Dick was alleged to have chopped off the arms, legs, and head of her spouse, leaving only his torso intact.

Trading Bentley to Toronto Called Hawks' Biggest Mistake

IN the '40s, the Chicago Blackhawks unveiled the "Pony Line" — Max Bentley, brother Doug, and Bill Mosienko. They were a darting, dynamic combo, good enough for all three to skate into the Hockey Hall of Fame. In 1947, Conn Smythe forced the breakup of the line through a bold deal that the Hawks just couldn't refuse.

Smythe coveted 27-year-old Max Bentley and offered Chicago five players in return for him: Bob Goldham, Bud Poile, Gus Bodnar, Gaye Stewart, and Ernie Dickens. It was the deal of the decade and one Chicago would later regret making. It took the club years to regain the fan support lost when Chicagoans became enraged at Bentley's departure. Bentley told Rex MacLeod of the *Toronto Star*,

The deal broke my father's heart. And it almost broke mine. I loved Chicago. We were both upset that Doug and I would be apart. Smythe would have taken Doug too but he was getting on — he was 31 that year. And someone told me Bill Tobin (Hawks manager) wanted 10 players from Smythe if Doug went with me.

We, dad and I, both felt better when Toronto won the Cup that year, beating Detroit four straight in the finals. Leafs won again the following year and again we beat the Wings four straight. We came back with another Cup win in '51. Those three Cup wins in four years made life in Toronto much more pleasant.

After Leafs won the Cup in '48, Bill Tobin came to see me. He put his arm around me and said, "Max, trading you was the biggest mistake I made in my life. The Chicago crowd came to see you and your linemates play. Now attendance has fallen off and we finished in the league basement."

Bentley won the NHL scoring title with Chicago in the two years prior to his trade.

"But I didn't know anything about winning," he admitted, "until I came to the Leafs. That's something you must learn. You must have a good coach who knows what he is doing and we had one in Hap Day. Day was strict but he was smart and he knew the game. With Day, there was no monkey business in practice. I believe the way you practice is the way you play."

Max Bentley and Vic Lynn, two former Leafs, were discussing the Edmonton Oilers one night in the '80s. It was one of those seasons when Gretzky and his mates were setting records of 400+ goals per year. The two oldtimers were not impressed.

Max asked Vic how many goals the Oilers would have scored against their Cup-winning team of 1948, the team Conn Smythe called "the greatest hockey squad ever assembled."

Vic said, "Probably none. Certainly no more than two. And

by then we'd have scored 15 against them. Remember, Max, we were noted for our checking but we could throw the puck in the net, too."

The late Dick Beddoes added a little fuel to the debate by stating, "Gretzky would be a fourth line centre on a Leaf team that had Apps, Kennedy, and Bentley on the roster."

With all due respect to the opinions of Bentley, Lynn, and Beddoes, it's my opinion that one of today's super teams would blow the 1948 Leafs out of the arena. Today's NHLers skate faster, shoot harder, and display skills that few oldtimers mastered. As for the Beddoes comment about Gretzky, neither Apps, Kennedy, nor Bentley, brilliant as they were, would be likely to overshadow the Great One in his prime.

Two Nags and a Caddie for Max

O NE reason Max Bentley was disappointed with the trade that brought him from Chicago to Toronto in 1947 was the loss of a new car — a Cadillac. Blackhawk president Bill Tobin had promised the two-time NHL scoring champion that he would give him a new Cadillac if he could win the Art Ross Trophy three times in a row.

Then came the trade to the Leafs, where Max had difficulty fitting in with his new club at first. His scoring touch temporarily deserted him and he finished fifth in scoring, behind Elmer Lach, Buddy O'Connor, brother Doug Bentley, and Gaye Stewart.

"I'll never forget that season and how much I wanted that Cadillac," Max would tell people in his retirement years.

Somehow word of his lost reward reached Leaf owner Conn Smythe. When Max was in Toronto to be inducted into the

Hockey Hall of Fame in 1966, Smythe presented him with the keys to a gleaming new Cadillac.

During his playing career as a Leaf, two admiring team supporters provided Max with some horsepower of a different kind. The Leafs fell behind Detroit 2–1 one night when there was a delay in the action. A wealthy fan shouted at Max, "Tie the score, Max, and I'll give you one of my race horses." Seconds later, Max scored. A Gardens director heard about the four-legged gift and presented Max with a second horse. Max ran the horses in Western Canada and made a few bucks on them before they were lost in claiming races.

Max Bentley scored 245 goals in 646 NHL games. His brother Doug potted 219 as a Chicago Blackhawk. A third brother, Reg, played briefly with Chicago and in later years could brag that, between them, the Bentley boys accounted for 465 NHL goals. Reg scored one.

Day Rewrites Record Book

BY the end of the 1948–49 NHL season, coach Clarence "Hap" Day had an enviable coaching record in hockey — in fact, a record-breaking one. In nine seasons behind the Leaf bench, he had captured five Stanley Cups.

In 1941–42, his Leafs made history by losing the first three games of the final series to Detroit, then storming back to take four in a row to capture the Cup.

In 1944–45, Day used only "eleven good men and true" to end the Montreal Canadiens' reign.

Then came his grand-slam feat, with victories in '47, '48, and '49.

If the Leafs had won again in 1950, Day might have been the first coach to lead his team to five consecutive Cup triumphs, for Toronto won again in '51 on Barilko's memorable goal. But Day's Leafs finished third in the standings in 1949–50, behind second-place Montreal and first-place Detroit. The Wings' big line of Lindsay, Abel, and Howe finished 1–2–3 in the scoring race, with Lindsay taking the Art Ross Trophy. The Leafs trounced Detroit 5–0 in the opening game of the semifinals, a game in which Howe suffered a devastating injury. When Ted Kennedy slipped away from a Howe check, the big right winger slammed head-first into the boards and suffered a concussion, a broken nose, a scratched eyeball, and a broken cheekbone. Despite the loss of Howe, the Wings fought back and eliminated Toronto in seven games. They went on to edge the Rangers in the finals.

By then, Hap Day had had enough of the pressures of coaching. He quit as the Leaf mentor in 1950 but stayed with the team for another seven years as assistant manager and manager. But he wasn't happy in the role. His self-esteem suffered working for Conn Smythe, who made most of the major decisions. Day was never comfortable playing a subservient position so he resigned in 1957.

"I was glad to get away from it," he said at the time. "I would have dug ditches rather than stay with the game."

Day was one of the toughest coaches ever to handle the Leafs. His training camps were described as prison camps. Pity the poor Leaf who made mistakes in practice. Day would jump all over him. He believed in defensive hockey and opponents complained that his Leafs were nothing more than clutch-and-grab artists. His players may have cursed him (behind his back, of course), but they agreed he knew what he was doing at all times and he knew how to get the best out of them. What better endorsement can a coach receive? Day kept his promise to forget hockey when he left the Leafs. He purchased a company that produced axe and tool handles and swept those memorable championship seasons almost completely out of his mind. He was inducted into the Hockey Hall of Fame in 1961.

Kennedy Blamed
for Howe Injury

IN the spring of 1949, Toronto's Hap Day established a remarkable coaching record with his fifth Stanley Cup championship in nine seasons. In the finals against Detroit the Red Wings even gasped oxygen from a tank near their bench in a desperate move to topple the Leafs.

The following spring the two clubs met again, this time in the semifinals. Who could blame the Wings if they lacked confidence? The Leafs, after all, had defeated them in 11 straight playoff games and had knocked them out of contention for three consecutive seasons.

In the opener, a 5–0 shutout for the Leafs, young Gordie Howe, Detroit's leading goal scorer, suffered a devastating injury. Howe was rushed to a Detroit hospital, where preliminary examinations brought discouraging news. Howe had a deep cut near his right eye, a fractured nose and cheekbone, and a severe concussion. After a team of doctors performed a 90-minute operation to relieve pressure from a broken blood vessel in his head, possibly saving his life, Howe's condition improved. It was described as "serious" but according to one surgeon, "The outlook is good." A few days later he was out of danger and he made a speedy recovery.

There were conflicting opinions as to how the injury had occurred. Many Detroit fans blamed the Leafs' Ted Kennedy. They said he deliberately sent Howe crashing into the boards head first. Toronto representatives said it was an accident, that Howe lunged at Kennedy, lost his balance and tumbled into the boards. Kennedy did not receive a penalty on the play and the game officials absolved him of any blame.

Kennedy was a marked man in game two. He finished the contest with assorted cuts and bruises including a black eye and a split lip. The Wings bludgeoned their way to a 3–1 victory in one of the roughest, bloodiest playoff games in NHL history.

The series ended in overtime in the seventh game, won by Detroit on a long shot by defenceman Leo Reise. The Leafs' long mastery over the Red Wings was finally over.

Even so, the hockey season was not over at the Gardens. Detroit faced the New York Rangers in the 1950 finals and with the circus taking over Madison Square Garden, the Rangers opted to play their "home" games in Toronto. The series went the limit and was decided on a goal by the Wings' Pete Babando in the second overtime period.

Don't Get Watson Mad!

WHEN husky Harry Watson patrolled left wing for the Leafs in the '40s and '50s, he was given a wide berth by many of hockey's so-called tough guys. The word was out: Don't mess with Harry! Oddly enough, the man who earned the greatest fear and respect from his opponents was one of the most even-tempered, mild-mannered players in league history. Watson seldom drew a penalty and was always a candidate for the Lady Byng Trophy because of his clean, disciplined play.

Watson's reputation as a man to be feared was established early in his career, during a game in Boston. Watson and the Bruins' Murray Henderson, another pacifist and a player who would later become one of Watson's best friends, exchanged body-checks. A few words followed and tempers flared. Then the gloves came off.

Watson's fists lashed out and Henderson's nose and face caught most of the punches. His nose was broken, his cheeks were bruised and bloodied. The broken beak led to two black eyes and Henderson, in profile at least, never looked the same again.

Watson became the talk of the league, hailed as the new heavyweight champ of hockey. And he remained that way, almost unchallenged, until he retired after 14 seasons. After the Henderson fight, coaches cautioned their players, "Don't get that Watson mad. He'll murder you."

Harry Watson was inducted into the Hockey Hall of Fame in 1994. It was recognition long overdue for his splendid play on the ice over 14 NHL seasons, almost nine of them with the Leafs. If a group of oldtime players hadn't noticed the oversight, and drawn up a petition listing Harry's credentials and calling for his nomination, I wonder if he'd have ever known the thrill that goes with becoming an honoured member of the Hall. Harry scored 236 goals in 809 career games.

Father Les

HE played only 15 games with the Leafs in a three-year span, scoring two goals and three assists for five points. His playoff stats were better — four points in six postseason games. As a rookie Leaf in 1947–48, he saw enough playing time to get his name engraved on the Stanley Cup. How many 15-game players can match that?

He's Les Costello, another of those tough young kids from South Porcupine in Northern Ontario who left home at age 15 to enroll at St. Michael's College in Toronto. There a solid education was waiting for the dedicated student and a possible career in hockey enticed the student athlete.

Costello learned his lessons well. He came under the scholastic influence of Fathers Mallen, MacIntyre, and David Bauer. In time the priesthood would beckon but so would professional hockey.

He turned pro in 1947 and played with Toronto and the club's farm team in Pittsburgh. But he was unsettled and unsure if he'd chosen the right path in life, so he decided to turn his back on the game as a career. He entered a seminary and four years later emerged as Father Les Costello. He told me once, "In the Catholic religion we believe that God selects the ones he wants to be priests, we don't choose him. Why he picks the people he does, we just don't know.

"It's not unlike your wife choosing you, Brian. She probably doesn't know why. She could have picked somebody good looking and rich, ha, ha, ha."

This was after a charity hockey game at Maple Leaf Gardens between the Flying Fathers team and the NHL Oldtimers. For years, Father Les had been the star of the Flying Fathers, a remarkable team of priests who'd entertained fans from coast to coast and overseas as well.

"Our motto is, Playing and praying — for a better world," explained Father Les. "If you can help the people to get away from their troubles for an hour or two, if they can enjoy a good laugh at our antics on the ice and we can raise a few dollars for charity, then it's a very good Christian philosophy, don't you think? Like tonight, I understand we helped raise $225,000 for the Charlie Conacher Cancer Fund. It was wonderful to see Frank Mahovlich and Dick Duff out there playing against us.

"And Brian, you still have your title, Bishop McFarlane. Remember you played for us in Moncton a few years back and scored three goals. If you'd scored another we'd have made you a Cardinal."

"Father Les," I said, "tell our readers that story you told me on CBC Radio once about your long-awaited trip to the Vatican."

He laughs. "Well, that was back in 1972 when the Flying Fathers played overseas and we took a trip to the Vatican to visit Pope Paul VI. We were sitting up in front at St. Peter's and for some reason we were introduced to the congregation as retired army chaplains from Canada.

"Then the Holy Father came right down and talked to us — Father McKee, Father Scanlan, and myself.

"So I stood up and presented him with a gift — a hockey stick

— one of our best models. And when he held it up and looked at it rather quizzically, I laughed and said, 'Well, if you don't know what to do with it you can always use it to stir spaghetti.' And that's a true story.

"Later, while everyone was milling around, I went up and sat in the Holy Father's chair. Just to see what it was like. Well, when I sat down a hush fell over St. Peter's. I was just about to give the Pope a little blessing when the Swiss guards came rushing over and hustled me out of there. They said, 'Holy place, father. Get out of here!' So my little *faux pas* may have set the Catholic Church in Canada back about 200 years, Brian. I'm afraid there won't be a Canadian Pope for a little while, anyway. Ha, ha, ha."

Traded for a Press Box

NORMAN "Bud" Poile was 18 when he signed with the Leafs for $1,500 in 1942. Poile not only changed sweater numbers often (with the Leafs he was 7, 11, 16, and 25) he switched teams as frequently. In 1947 he was part of the huge trade with Chicago that brought Max Bentley to the Leafs. Despite his 20-goal average per season over the next three years, he moved from Chicago to Detroit to New York to Boston. The only team sweater he didn't get to wear was Montreal's.

"I forget all the players I was traded for," says Poile. "But one year I was traded for a press box. Detroit swapped me to New York for $35,000. They told me they were building a new press box in the Olympia and they needed the money they could get for me to build it."

THE FIFTIES

Hainsworth Killed in Head-On Highway Crash

GEORGE Hainsworth, a member of two Stanley Cup–winning teams and a three-time winner of the Vezina Trophy, was killed instantly on the night of October 9, 1950, in a head-on collision between his car and a truck south of Gravenhurst, Ontario. Hainsworth, who joined the Toronto Maple Leafs from Montreal in a trade for goalie Lorne Chabot in 1933, was pronounced dead at the scene of the accident. Medical experts said several broken ribs had punctured his heart.

During his three seasons with the Leafs, Hainsworth helped guide his club to two league championships. But he'll forever be remembered for the 1928–29 season, when he played for the Montreal Canadiens. That year he compiled 22 shutouts in 44 games and posted a 0.98 goals-against average, allowing a mere 43 goals during the season. In 11 seasons (and 464 games) he recorded 94 shutouts, only nine fewer than Terry Sawchuk's career mark of 103. Sawchuk required 21 seasons (and 971 games) to establish the record.

At the time of his death, the 54-year-old Toronto-born Hall of Fame netminder was an alderman in his adopted city of Kitchener, Ontario.

Triumphs and Troubles
of the Turkey Man

EAF owner Conn Smythe once said, "If we had to play one game with everything at stake, Turk Broda would be my goaltender."

Smythe first saw the 21-year-old Broda play goal in the spring of 1936. Smythe had watched in disgust as Leaf goalie George Hainsworth gave up nine goals in a playoff game to Detroit. Smythe decided it was time to find a replacement for the beleaguered Hainsworth. The Leaf owner stayed in Detroit to scout Earl Robertson, a Detroit sub netminder with a "can't miss" reputation. Robertson was playing for the Detroit Bulldogs in a game against the Detroit Olympics. During the contest it wasn't the Bulldogs' Robertson who impressed Smythe. Instead, the burly goalie on the Olympics caught Smythe's eye — a 21-year-old from Brandon, Manitoba, named Walter "Turk" Broda. The nickname Turk, Smythe soon learned, came from Broda's childhood pals, who claimed that Broda's freckles reminded them of a turkey egg.

The Red Wings, who sponsored both the Olympics and the Bulldogs, said they'd be happy to part with Broda for the sum of $8,000. If Smythe couldn't see that Robertson was a much better prospect, that was his problem. The Wings' Jack Adams had no qualms about taking money from a blind man. Smythe anted up and bought himself a future Hall-of-Famer.

At first Smythe's cronies questioned his decision. Broda, they pointed out, looks and acts kind of funny. He's a yappy guy and he's got the appetite of a horse. Now that he's earning a big-league salary he'll eat himself out of the league in no time. Look at that body! Really, Conn, the man is fat! A few more doughnuts and he won't be able to lace up his skates.

Conn Smythe smiled and said, "Let's just wait and see."

It didn't take long for the roly-poly Broda to establish himself as one of the game's best puck stoppers. At the same time he became one of hockey's most popular players. From 1936 to 1952, he played in 628 games for the Leafs and recorded 62 shutouts. He played in 101 Stanley Cup playoff games, a record at the time, and chalked up 13 playoff shutouts, another record. He won the Vezina Trophy twice, with a 2.06 average in 1940–41 and a 2.38 average in 1947–48. His 1948 Vezina prevented Montreal's Bill Durnan from capturing the trophy seven times in a row.

Broda led the Leafs to five Stanley Cups, including four in five years in the late 1940s. His work in the playoffs was often spectacular and even today he is named by oldtimers as one of hockey's greatest "money" goaltenders.

In the 1949 Stanley Cup final series against Detroit, Broda allowed just five goals in four games as the Leafs swept the Red Wings aside for their third straight Cup triumph.

In 1951, at age 37, he allowed just nine goals in eight games as Toronto won the Cup again, this time on Bill Barilko's memorable overtime goal against Montreal.

Smythe held a "night" for Broda on December 22, 1951. Only one other Leaf — King Clancy — had been honoured in such a manner. It was Broda's last season. He played in only one game during the regular schedule, but after Al Rollins lost the opening game of the playoff series with Detroit, Turk heard the call. In game two he played brilliantly, only to lose 1–0 in his 100th playoff start. He started again in game three against the Wings and was shelled 6–2. Rollins finished up as the Leafs bowed out in four games.

In retirement, Broda turned to coaching. His travels took him to Quebec City, Moncton, Charlotte, N.C., and Newmarket. He found his coaching niche in junior hockey and his Toronto Marlboros won two Memorial Cups in the fifties. He yearned for a crack at the NHL, and it was thought he might find himself behind the Leaf bench one day. Three times the position became open, and three times he was said to be "not quite right" for the job — passed over in favour of Howie Meeker, Billy Reay, and Punch Imlach.

In his 50s his health began to fail. His marriage came apart. His final and biggest thrill in hockey was being named to the Hockey Hall of Fame in 1967, Canada's centennial year. Five years later he died of a heart attack.

Sportswriter Rick Boulton tells the story of Broda's daughter and some of her friends returning from a rock concert one night, a few weeks before he passed away. "'Mr. Broda,' said one of the teenagers, 'you never heard such a noise at Maple Leaf Gardens.'

'Oh yes, I have,' he grinned in reply."

Smythe Saw Hockey on TV Before Anyone Else

IN October 1951, the CBC began assembling a staff to televise hockey games from Maple Leaf Gardens. The producer was a former Winnipegger named George Retzlaff. For the first eight weeks of the 1951–52 NHL season, Leaf games were televised but "in private." They were really dry runs, for the personal viewing of one man, owner Conn Smythe. Smythe wanted to be sure that television was going to be a suitable medium for hockey and he wouldn't give the CBC the green light until he was satisfied.

The first game televised, early in 1952, was an instant success with viewers and hockey was soon the highest-rated show on television.

But Retzlaff had to deal with Smythe, who insisted that the cameras must not block a paying fan's view. Retzlaff was forced to place them on a single platform, high up near the roof of the Gardens.

It was two years before he persuaded Smythe to allow him to move two cameras into the green seat section, displacing several seats and the cash customers who normally occupied them.

It took another few months before he was allowed to place a

camera at ice level on the west side of the Gardens. Again, more cash customers were evicted.

Retzlaff soon made another request. Could the camera in the studio be trundled out during the periods and shoot the game in progress — from ice level? At first Smythe said absolutely not, but Retzlaff persisted and finally the owner reluctantly agreed. "Just make sure your cameraman doesn't bother any of the spectators," growled Smythe.

On the first night the studio camera was wheeled close to rinkside, there was a man standing in behind the Leaf bench blocking the shot in the cameraman's viewfinder. "Hey, buddy!" he yelled. "Get the hell out of the way. You're in my shot."

The man turned around and it was Smythe. Retzlaff, watching on a monitor in the TV truck, groaned. He saw Smythe's lips moving and his finger wagging in the direction of the camera. Within seconds the CBC cameraman was back in the studio with Smythe's edict ringing in his ears. "Back that thing out of here and never bring it back."

Brewer Was a Rebel

(O)NE night during the 1959–60 season, Leaf defenceman Carl Brewer said a few unkind words about referee Eddie Powers. Powers overheard every adjective and sentenced Brewer to the penalty box to cool off. The period ended with Brewer still serving his time. But when the penalty timekeepers got up to leave the box, they got a surprise. Brewer had locked the penalty box door and refused to let them out. Hot words were exchanged and a scuffle ensued. Brewer's behaviour was noted on the referee's report to NHL headquarters, and it cost him a stiff fine.

It was a Brewer brainwave that led to the insertion of a new rule in the referee's handy guide to officiating. After a battle on Toronto ice one night, referee Vern Buffey spotted a pair of unusual gloves on the ice, tossed there by one of the combatants. The palms had been removed from each glove, and when Brewer skated over to retrieve them, Buffey had the answer to a long-standing mystery. How, he had often wondered, was Brewer able to throw opposing forwards off stride so easily when they fought for space in front of the Leaf goal crease? The answer lay in the palmless gloves. Brewer simply reached through the holes, clutched an opponent by the jersey, and tossed him around like a rag doll.

For the following season there was a new rule in the book: Players could no longer perform with palmless hockey gloves.

In my Hockey Museum in Niagara Falls, Ontario, I have a pair of palmless hockey gloves donated by former NHL defenceman Ivan Irwin, my teammate during Sunday morning scrimmages. Irwin claims to have used the "doctored" gloves to clutch unwary opponents and avoid detection many years before Brewer arrived in the NHL.

———————

Had Brewer not been such a rebel, and had he played longer in the NHL, he might easily have compiled career marks that would have led to his entry into the Hockey Hall of Fame. As one who knows him well, if that's possible, I suggest he couldn't care less about such recognition, just as he has turned down offers to write a book about his interesting career. His major contribution to hockey, and every player should thank him for it, was his stubborn resolve to battle the league in the great pension dispute of 1994 — eventually winning the costly dispute — for millions of dollars in surplus funds owed to the retired players.

Free Agency:
Brewer Created His Own

H E'S been called unpredictable, an enigma, a flake, and a free spirit. He's Carl Brewer, who played for the Leafs from 1957–58 to 1964–65, during an era when hockey players were underpaid and strictly controlled. The owner or general manager wielded the power and the player was expected to snap to attention and say "Yes, sir" whenever an order was given.

Not Brewer, though. Because there was no free agency in the '60s, he simply created his own. Frustrated and fed up with the dictatorial style of Punch Imlach, he quit the Leafs in 1965. After Brewer quarrelled with Johnny Bower during a preseason game, Imlach told him, "If you're not going to stick up for Bower, your teammate, you can take off your uniform and go home." Brewer turned in his uniform and walked out. He fought for and regained his amateur standing and surfaced with Canada's national team. He played and coached overseas. Then there were stops in Muskegon (where he was paid a major league salary as player-coach), Detroit, and St. Louis. The Red Wings had acquired his rights as part of a blockbuster deal, one that brought them Frank Mahovlich, Garry Unger, and Pete Stemkowski in return for Norm Ullman, Paul Henderson, and Floyd Smith. John Zeigler, then an attorney for the Red Wings, signed him to a contract just minutes before his NHL rights would have reverted to Toronto. Brewer received a base salary of $92,000 plus bonuses that amounted to a potential $130,000. That's when Red Wing defenceman Bobby Baun took Gordie Howe for lunch and told him to get wise. "Gordie," he said. "I know you're making about $45,000 and I'm making a hell of a lot more than that. What'll really tick you off is to learn that Brewer's making more than both of us."

He left the Wings over "a matter of principle" and months later I ran into him, playing a game of shinny at Doublerinks in

Toronto. In the dressing room he casually mentioned that he was making another comeback — this time with St. Louis. A knee injury ended his playing time there and after a whirl with the Toronto Toros of the WHA he packed his skates away again.

But once more, at the ripe old age of 41, he succumbed to the persuasive voice of Punch Imlach, his old nemesis, and rejoined the Leafs during a time of need.

Brewer's brief swan song with the Leafs late in 1979, after 14 years' absence from the Gardens, was Imlach's idea. But the other Leafs branded Brewer an Imlach spy and ostracized him. Dave Hutchison and others took a few whacks at him in practice and Borje Salming decided he'd rather eat the puck than pass it to Brewer.

One night, after a Leaf charter flight returned the team to Pearson International Airport, Brewer and Imlach were huddled around Imlach's car, which wouldn't start. Punch had left the lights on when he parked, a fact one of the players had noticed and gleefully informed his teammates of — but not Imlach. When asked for assistance, several players denied having jumper cables, then drove away laughing. One of them even dangled a set of cables out of his car window as he drove by the stranded pair.

Later, Brewer and Imlach had another confrontation — this time over salary. Brewer sued Imlach and the Leafs, claiming he'd not been paid some of the money Imlach had promised him. Brewer lost the suit but sued again on another financial matter and was awarded $45,000.

No stranger to the courtroom, Brewer had once claimed the rights to the Maple Leaf name, pointing out that over the years the club had failed to protect it. In court the Leafs were awarded their name but, according to Brewer, it cost the team over $300,000 in legal fees to guarantee its return.

When the NHL stonewalled him in his quest for information about surplus funds from the players' pension fund, Brewer again sought legal assistance. He hired lawyer Mark Zigler, recruited former stars like Gordie Howe, Allan Stanley, Eddie Shack, and Andy Bathgate, and forced the league to answer in court. The result? A ruling that directed the NHL to fork over approximately $40 million to about a thousand former players. The ruling crushed former NHLPA executive director Alan Eagleson, who had maintained all along that any surpluses from the NHL pension fund belonged to the owners, not the players he represented.

Once dismissed as little more than an annoying activist, Brewer is now regarded by NHL moguls as a walking time bomb, a potential threat to their financial stability and their future. When he talks about his next possible target — investigating collusion among the owners (baseball has already been found guilty of such charges) — a shudder sweeps through every front office and Tylenol sales in NHL markets skyrocket.

Brewer often joins us for Sunday morning oldtimer scrimmages in Pickering, east of Toronto. He still handles the puck with magic hands. "I've always been known as a guy who likes tilting at windmills," he told me recently. "Why should I stop now?"

When someone congratulated him for his efforts on behalf of all the former NHLers, he laughed. "Why, that's just a start," he said. "Just the tip of the iceberg."

"Would you like to collaborate on a book about your amazing career in hockey?" I asked him.

He smiled and said, "No, I don't think so. Writing about myself is something that has never really interested me."

Punch Imlach's Biggest Thrill

WHEN a relatively unknown hockey vagabond named George "Punch" Imlach was hired as Toronto Maple Leaf assistant general manager in 1958, the job description puzzled him. He had nobody to assist, because the club had no general manager. King Clancy was in the executive suite but he too bore the title assistant general manager. And Clancy made it clear he had no ambitions to become anything else. Newcomer Imlach and oldtimer Clancy both might have been assisting Billy Reay, who had coached the Leafs to a dismal last-place finish in his rookie season in 1957–58. But when owner Conn Smythe had offered Reay the general manager's job a few weeks earlier, Reay had turned it down.

"I'd rather be the team coach," explained Reay. "I've got something to prove here."

Imlach soon found out how well known he was around Maple Leaf Gardens. When he went to the office receptionist and asked her to find Billy Reay, she said, "He's not in yet, sir. Care to take a seat and wait?"

The Leaf players didn't know who he was either. They'd heard that some bald, 40-year-old former senior player who'd been working in Springfield, Massachusetts, had been hired in an executive capacity, but they had no inkling what an impact he would soon have on their lives and careers.

When the Leafs won only five of their first 16 games in 1958, Imlach was asked by the Silver Seven, a group of directors, to explain the reason for the club's poor start. His response so impressed them that Imlach was asked to step right into the general manager's job. The team promptly lost four more games and Imlach decided he had no choice but to fire Reay, even though the coach was a favourite of team owner Conn Smythe.

He decided to coach the team himself, at least on an interim basis, and after a 2–1 loss to Chicago the following night, the players picked themselves up and went on a six-game undefeated streak. Imlach began telling everyone who'd listen that his last-place team was now inspired and would make the playoffs. Most of his listeners scoffed at the words of this cocky little optimist.

Imlach still considered himself a fill-in coach and within days offered the job to former NHL star Alf Pike. But Pike wanted certain conditions written into his contract, demands that took him out of the running and convinced Imlach he should remain behind the bench.

The new coach was pleased with his goaltending, having signed Johnny Bower to a contract as one of his first moves after joining the Toronto organization. Bower, acquired from Cleve-

Clarence Campbell presents Turk Broda with the richly deserved Vezina Trophy in 1951.
— Hockey Hall of Fame

Toronto goalie Harry Lumley in a duel with Bill Dineen of Detroit.
— Hockey Hall of Fame

The entire Leaf team looks on as Rocket Richard completes a hat trick for Montreal.
— Hockey Hall of Fame

The enduring King Clancy: from player to referee to coach to assistant general manager to "vice-president in charge of nothing."
— Hockey Hall of Fame

Conn Smythe hated the idea of an NHL players' union.
— Hockey Hall of Fame

After Carl Brewer quit the Leafs in 1965, he became a free agent in an era when most players were strictly controlled. — Hockey Hall of Fame

Leonard (Red) Kelly goes for a fall behind the Canadiens' net. — Hockey Hall of Fame

Leaf captain George Armstrong scores on Boston's Ed Johnston. — Hockey Hall of Fame

Hot Stove League: Bobby Hewitson, Jack Dennett, Baldy Cotton, Wes McKnight, and Syl Apps. — Chris Lund/NFB/National Archives of Canada/PA-111477

Armstrong, Bentley, and Lewicki ham it up on a couch. — Hockey Hall of Fame

Toronto goalie Johnny Bower thwarts the Bruins' Johnny Bucyk. — Hockey Hall of Fame

Frank Mahovlich after a four-goal night; he finished his career with 533 goals and 1,103 points.
— Hockey Hall of Fame

Veteran Jacques Plante had eight Vezina trophies to his name when he came to Toronto in 1970.

Paul Henderson will always be best remembered for his winning goal for Team Canada against the Soviets in 1972.

Four comebacks were one too many for Tim Horton, whose career ended tragically with his fatal 1974 car crash.
— Robert B. Shaver

The author with Punch Imlach on NBC. — Robert B. Shaver

Darryl Sittler's 1976 10-point game still stands unmatched.
— Robert B. Shaver

*For better or for worse,
Harold Ballard ruled
Maple Leaf Gardens for
two decades.*

Swedish import Borje Salming anchored the Toronto defence for over 1,000 games.
— Robert B. Shaver

land in the off-season, was proving to be a standout at age 33. Imlach bolstered his defence by turning Carl Brewer pro and picking up Allan Stanley from Boston in return for Jim Morrison. Midway through the season, the Bruins placed Larry Regan on waivers and Imlach claimed him. Regan, a clever playmaker, became the ideal centreman for Dick Duff and George Armstrong. He traded minor leaguer Willie Marshall to Hershey for Gerry Ehman, who'd scored 40 goals for Imlach in Springfield the previous season. Ehman turned out to be a very productive forward.

Despite the canny moves, by mid-March Imlach's Leafs were still long shots for a playoff berth. Time was running out and they were nine points away from the fourth place New York Rangers. At about that time, Wes McKnight, sports director of Toronto radio station CFRB, assigned a young broadcaster named McFarlane to interview Ranger coach Phil Watson for a show called *Meet the Hockey Stars*. When McFarlane popped the big question, "Coach, is there any chance the Leafs can overtake your club in the race to the playoffs?" Watson scowled and said, "Young fella, there's no way that's gonna happen. No way! And you can tell Imlach his club will never put my team out of the playoffs. In fact, I'm going to keep his team out of the playoffs. And that's the truth!"

The NHL offices, then located in Montreal, began releasing possible playoff matchups for the television people and the newspapers. There was no mention of Toronto in any of the matchups. Obviously even the league executives thought it was preposterous to consider the Leafs for any postseason activity.

With two weeks to play, the Leafs met the Rangers in back-to-back games. On Saturday, March 14, at Maple Leaf Gardens, Toronto blanked New York 5–0, and then held on the following night to win a thrilling game 6–5 back in New York. Both were "must-win" games for Imlach and the Leafs. Now Imlach's men were only three points behind Watson's club with three games left to play.

The following Thursday the Leafs went into the Montreal Forum and defeated the Canadiens 6–3. Now they were only one point back of New York, for the Rangers had lost to the Bruins the previous night.

On Saturday afternoon (the final weekend), the Rangers re-grouped and beat Detroit 5–2 to re-establish a three-point cushion over Toronto. But the Leafs downed Chicago 5–1 that night on home ice, which meant the race would go down to the final Sunday — with Toronto at Detroit and New York hosting Montreal.

Imlach had spent a sleepless night on the train ride to Detroit for the final encounter. At the old Detroit Olympia before game time, his heart flipped when he learned that the Rangers had jumped into an early lead over Montreal in their clash at Madison Square Garden. His pulse almost returned to normal when a followup report indicated the Habs were leading 2–1 after goals by Moore and Beliveau.

His next jolt came after the puck was dropped in Detroit. Two Red Wings, Norm Ullman and Marcel Pronovost, scored first-period goals against his Leafs to open up a two-goal lead. By then the final score had come in from New York: Montreal 4, Rangers 2. Punch rejoiced. There was still a chance. A Toronto win would cap one of the most incredible seasons in hockey history.

While he paced nervously outside the dressing room after the first period, Imlach was approached by Stafford Smythe. "Well, our boys gave it everything they had," said Smythe. "They've got nothing to be ashamed of."

"Stafford, don't be stupid," snarled Imlach. "We're not through yet. We're not going to lose this game. There's still forty minutes left."

Regan scored a pretty goal early in the second period and then Baun batted one in — his first goal of the season. Ullman scored another Red Wing goal, but Brewer quickly tied it with a blast. Then Regan, enjoying the best game of his career, put the Leafs ahead 4–3. But Pronovost made another nifty rush and fired the puck off Bower's glove into the net. With 20 minutes to play the score was tied 4–4.

In the third period Regan displayed some marvellous stick-handling and set up Dick Duff for his 29th goal of the season and the Leafs took a 5–4 lead. Regan said later, "I told Duffie I'd set him up for the winner." The insurance marker was engineered by another smooth stickhandler, Billy Harris. Harris manoeuvred the puck to Baun, who fired it toward the Detroit net. Harris deftly tipped it out of the air and into the cage to complete the scoring. Toronto 6, Detroit 4. The Leafs were in the playoffs, edging the Rangers by a single point.

Imlach always claimed that this was one of the greatest games he'd ever been involved in. "People love to see a team come from nowhere to accomplish something and that's what we did in my first year with Toronto," he said. "They called us the Cinderella Leafs because we got off the floor and started winning and we refused to quit. People love that sort of thing."

When the playoffs got underway, Imlach predicted his Leafs would win the first round against Boston — and they did, even after falling behind 2–0 in games. Gerry Ehman scored six goals in the seven-game series.

But Imlach's crystal ball let him down in the finals against Montreal. His team came close. The Cinderella Leafs were a constant threat to the mighty Habs, a club that was establishing a streak of five consecutive Stanley Cup triumphs. Montreal won the first two games on home ice by 5–3 and 3–1 scores. Back in Toronto the Leafs captured game three 3–2, and they might have won game four but for an unfortunate twist of fate, a bizarre playoff oddity. George Armstrong's hard shot went right through the webbing in Jacques Plante's net and the light failed to go on. Had the Leafs won that game (they lost 3–2) they would have returned to the Montreal Forum tied 2–2 instead of down 3–1. The Habs won game five and the Stanley Cup by a 5–3 score.

By then Imlach was not only a fixture in Toronto, he was famous. He would be back to lead his Leafs to the Stanley Cup four times in the '60s. But even after those stirring triumphs, he'd often look back with pride on the 1958–59 season and the dramatic victory over Detroit that won his team a surprise playoff berth.

"I can recall how every one of those goals was scored that night," he'd tell reporters. "Those goals, that game, and that season, provided me with the greatest thrill I've ever experienced in hockey."

Ankle Injury
Leads Kelly to Leafs

THROUGHOUT the 1950s, Leonard (Red) Kelly of the Red Wings was arguably the NHL's top rushing defenceman. He was a fixture in Detroit, a Norris Trophy winner and a three-time winner of the Lady Byng Trophy, and his name had been etched on the Stanley Cup on four occasions.

During the 1959–60 season, Kelly suffered an ankle injury that slowed him down. His boss, Jack Adams, asked him to hide the injury and Kelly obediently refrained from discussing it. Later, Adams concluded the injury had curtailed Kelly's natural speed. Or perhaps the redhead was just growing old. Now would be a good time to trade him. The Rangers were interested and coughed up Bill Gadsby and Eddie Shack for Kelly and Billy McNeill.

But Kelly refused to accept the deal and retired instead of reporting to New York. Two days later he was out of hockey and employed by a business firm in Detroit.

NHL president Clarence Campbell called him. "You'd better reconsider, young man," he told Kelly. "If you don't report to New York you'll be blackballed from hockey forever."

Campbell should have known better than to threaten a stubborn Irishman. "That's fine, Mr. Campbell," said Red. "I've had a dozen good years in the game and that should be enough for anyone."

The next day there was a call from King Clancy of the Leafs. He got Red's bride on the phone. "Andra, you'll let me speak to your husband, won't you?"

"I would, Mr. Clancy, but he's gone to work. Red started his new job today."

Clancy tracked Red down. He said, "Red, Punch Imlach has always liked you and we've got permission from Mr. Adams to talk to you. How about coming to Toronto for a meeting with Imlach?" Clancy's gift for the gab soon had Red wavering on the retirement idea. As a former St. Mike's student, he'd always admired Clancy and the Leafs.

Red was asked to travel to Toronto incognito. Clancy promised to meet him at the airport.

When Kelly arrived Clancy almost missed him. Red's copper hair was hidden under a bowler hat and his coat collar was turned up. Clancy chuckled at the disguise and hustled Kelly to Maple Leaf Gardens in a limousine. Later that day Kelly agreed to the generous offer Imlach placed on the table. Imlach phoned Adams, who had already agreed to take journeyman defenceman Marc Reaume for Kelly if the redhead joined the Leafs. Adams was told the deal was a go.

Adams hung up, failing even to wish Kelly good luck.

Later still, Kelly, Imlach, and Clancy headed for a downtown restaurant. A few blocks from the Gardens, Jim Vipond, the sports editor of the *Globe and Mail*, passed within a few feet of their limo but failed to see the famous occupant sitting in the back seat and missed the scoop of the season.

At a secluded table in the restaurant, Kelly discovered he wasn't the only hockey notable in the establishment. Toronto had a home game against the Canadiens the following night, and to everyone's surprise the entire Montreal team, led by Rocket Richard, filed in and seated themselves nearby. Richard spotted Kelly and came over to say hello. But he quickly sensed that something important was going on. The Rocket smiled and placed a finger to his mouth, as if to say "My lips are sealed."

The next morning the acquisition of Kelly was front-page news. At the morning skate he posed for photographers wearing number 4. His wife, Andra, flew in from Detroit for the game with Montreal. She told me recently, "I couldn't believe the reception Red got from the Toronto fans. All that day, on the street, in the hotel, everybody was talking about my husband. Everybody seemed to know him. I was newly married and didn't realize what a big hero he was. I'd never seen anything like it."

Red said, "When Punch sent me over the boards to take my first shift the ovation I received was incredible. Punch played me at centre that night and I made up my mind I wouldn't let Beliveau beat me on the faceoff. I won it cleanly and flipped the puck into the Montreal zone. I charged after it . . . right into the Montreal goal crease. Their goalie must have seen the look in my eye because he took a dive and I did a full somersault right over him. Andra often talks about the somersault that got me started as a Leaf."

The deal for Kelly was the best trade Imlach ever made — by a long shot. The redhead went on to help the Leafs win four Stanley Cups, at an age when he should have been over the hill. He was inducted into the Hockey Hall of Fame in 1969. He even found time to combine hockey with politics, serving as a member of the federal Parliament, which required incredible energy and stamina.

5

THE SIXTIES

Another Classy Captain

DAVE Keon, like other Leaf captains before him (Kennedy, Apps, Armstrong, etc.), could do it all. He was a gifted goal scorer, a tireless skater, a relentless checker, a superb playmaker, and a leader who avoided the penalty box.

In 1960, he jumped from junior hockey at St. Michael's to the NHL, and won the Calder Trophy as rookie of the year in '61. In '62 he played on a Stanley Cup winner (his biggest thrill). His second biggest was capturing a fourth Cup win in '67 and being named MVP of the playoffs. He remains the only Leaf to win the Conn Smythe Trophy. "It was a wonderful time to be a Leaf," he says, "playing in the '60s and winning four Stanley Cups."

One of only five Leafs to play more than 1,000 NHL games, Keon set team records with 365 goals and 858 points. Both marks were later erased by another great captain, Darryl Sittler. He was twice awarded the Lady Byng Trophy for his gentlemanly play and rarely visited the penalty box. When Bobby Hull was barred from Team Canada in 1972 (because he'd jumped to the WHA), there was a storm of criticism. The furor over Hull's omission overshadowed the anger of Keon fans, who felt this great little player, who excelled in the "European style" of hockey, should have been selected. Jim Proudfoot, writing in the *Toronto Star*, said, "Keon is the most talented individual omitted from Team Canada."

Ballard Wields Big Axe

IN the mid-'60s, those of us who worked on *Hockey Night in Canada* were excited about a marvellous innovation: colour TV.

The technicalities had been worked out and thousands of dollars in new lights installed. The lights created so much candlepower that some of the players rubbed a black substance on their upper cheeks to cut down on the glare.

Before the first game Harold Ballard approached Ted Hough, head of *Hockey Night in Canada*, and a debate followed as to who was responsible for the cost of installing the new lights.

"I'm not paying so it's either you or your sponsors," roared Ballard. When Hough said he'd think about it, Ballard disappeared. He came back moments later wielding a big axe. He nodded at one of the TV cables on the floor.

"If you don't make a decision in five minutes I'm going to cut through this cable and there'll be no telecast of the game tonight," Ballard threatened.

Before he could hoist the axe, Hough had decided. His company would pay for the additional lighting.

Unpredictable Don Simmons

FORMER Leaf Billy Harris, in his book *The Glory Years*, recalls the night of Saturday, January 18, 1964. The Leafs, reigning Stanley Cup champions, were hosting the lowly Boston Bruins, a team of tanglefoots who were destined to finish dead last in the NHL standings.

Harris had a special reason for wanting his team to perform well that night. A friend from the Maritimes, Cam Lindsay, was sitting in seats that Harris had arranged, right up against the glass. Lindsay, a devoted Leaf fan all of his life, had finally made it to the Gardens to see his heroes play. It was a dream come true, and none too soon, for Lindsay was dying of cancer. During the warm-up his face lit up like a Christmas bulb every time Billy Harris skated past.

What a crushing disappointment it turned out to be for Lindsay when the Leafs fell flat on their fannies before a stone-cold crowd and lost the game by a shocking score, 11–0. His pal Harris sat on the Leaf bench for most of the game, and when Hinky finally saw some ice time late in the third — with his team trailing 9–0 — the Bruins promptly scored a tenth goal and the Harris line was yanked back to the bench. By then the fans were mocking goalie Don Simmons's every save and cheering every Boston goal. "We want more!" they shouted. "We want eleven!" And eleven they got, as Cam Lindsay shook his head in disbelief and Punch Imlach roared in anger.

Harris says Imlach seldom berated a player in front of his mates but the following day, during a team meeting prior to a game at the Chicago Stadium, he blistered Leaf goalie Don Simmons for his shoddy performance the night before.

"You'll never wear a Leaf uniform again," he told the embarrassed netminder. "I'm flyin' in Al Millar from the coast and he'll be in goal against the Hawks tonight."

But Millar didn't show. Foul weather had delayed his flight to Chicago. At the last minute Imlach had no choice but to toss the disgraced Simmons the same Leaf jersey he'd just promised him he'd never wear again. Simmons, who'd been found munching on a hot dog in the bowels of the Chicago Stadium 20 minutes before game time, had no chance for a warm-up. Still haunted by the 11–0 nightmare in Toronto and Imlach's pregame tirade, Simmons was neither mentally nor physically prepared to face the wicked shots of Bobby Hull, Stan Mikita, and company. A second consecutive humiliation appeared to be a certainty.

But Simmons amazed himself — and his mates — by standing up to every Chicago attack despite all the trauma he'd suffered in the past 24 hours. The Blackhawk snipers, who gleefully anticipated victimizing the shaken netminder for another 10 or 12 goals, were left fuming at Simmons's reversal of form. He blocked everything they threw at him and at game's end, grinning at the vagaries of a game that could turn a man into a goat one minute and a Goliath the next, he skated into the arms of his teammates after recording a stunning 2–0 shutout.

Don Simmons might not have been a Hall of Fame goaltender but he fashioned some respectable statistics in his 11-year NHL career, despite playing with some weak Boston clubs during his first five years in the league. He recorded 20 shutouts and a career goals-against average of 2.93 in 247 regular season games. In 24 playoff games his goals-against average was 2.67.

Shack Gets a Nickname

SOME time ago I was in Hamilton at a sports banquet and Eddie Shack was one of the guest speakers. He entertained the crowd with the following presentation:

> People often ask me how I got the name "Clear the Track." When I was with the Leafs we played New York one night and I smacked Rod Gilbert and another Ranger — both at the same time. They hit the ice and rolled around and I didn't even get a penalty. The late Paul Rimstead wrote about me the next day and the headline read: "Clear the Track, Here Comes Shack."
>   Then Brian McFarlane over there made up a song to go along with the name. He must have said "Holy sheepshit, maybe I can do somethin' with this." You

know, he's supposed to be a writer and he's got some books to prove it and all that. I don't think he knows shit about music but anyway he did it and it went to number one on the hit parade for the next few weeks.

It went like this:

Clear the track, here comes Shack,
He knocks them down, he gives 'em a whack,
He can score goals, he's found the knack,
Eddie, Eddie Shack.
He started the year in the minors,
And almost gave up the game,
Then boom! He's back with the big club
And the Leafs haven't quite been the same.

There was a lot more but that gives you the idea. Hey, it was true. I always spent the beginning of the year in the minors. With Imlach, if you misbehaved you were sent to the minors for a couple of weeks. So I was always going down. It was absolutely hell playing for Imlach. The lines were Keon, Armstrong and Duff. Then it was Kelly, Mahovlich and Nevin. Then it was Olmstead, Stewart and somebody else. After that it was always Shack and Harris and whoever the hell wants to play with them. That was Imlach. I didn't score many goals because I was always sitting on the bench. If I squawked, Imlach would say, "For Christ's sake, shuddup, Shack, or it will cost you ten bucks for a ticket to get in and watch the game."

Even so, the game of hockey has been great for me. I got to play with so many clubs. My little wifey — she's such a sweet little thing — told me we could make more damn money on our real estate deals moving from city to city than we could from hockey. She used to say, "Shackie, you better act up again and tick somebody off so we can get the hell out of here."

Hockey is fabulous. When I was with the Leafs and we were playing Montreal we always anticipated a scrap or two. The team was always up for those games. Well, most of us. I'd have to get Frank Mahovlich up for them because Frank could be in a bit of a cloud. I mean he's a great guy and everything but Jesus Christ! Get up Frank! And Imlach would love me for that.

In some of those games I always picked on their smallest guy — like Henri Richard. When you're a Ukrainian from Sudbury and you see a French guy out there, well, you just don't like him, see. You don't like the way he talks, you don't like how short he is, you don't like how fast he skates and you absolutely want to kick the shit out of him. So I get ahold of Henri and remember, the rule was the third man in is thrown out of the game. That was a great deal for me, especially with Ferguson always hanging around.

While I'm throwing Henri around — and he's a tough little sonofabitch — who comes nosing around but Ferguson. He wants to get at me. I can't shake Richard so I said to myself, let's see if the little bugger can take it. So I bonked him with my head. Boom! I hit him just above the eye and now the blood is coming down and the worst language is coming out of him, "Shit de shit de goddamn. My brudder from two and a 'aff rivers will kill you, Shack."

Now we have to go back and play at the Forum again and I'm a nervous wreck. In the warmup there's a guy blowing a big horn and chanting, "Shack the nose . . . Shack the nose!" And Fergie is shouting nasty things at me. I'm praying for a tie score because I know if one side grabs a big lead, Imlach is going to be saying, "All right, Shack and Harris and whoever the hell wants to go out there with them."

After the period, we go through the exit and who the hell is sitting up there but Maurice Richard, Henri's big brother. You know, the guy who got two minutes for looking so good on television. He cups a hand and yells at me. "Shack, thank God you didn't hit my brother with your big nose. You would have split him in two."

I don't know if the kids today have the fun that we

did. Hockey is a fun game. When I opened a hockey school I told the kids to push, grind and shoot the puck. I told them to hold the stick with both hands and skate with your head up. Of course I never did it myself, ha ha, but I told them to do it.

I also told them that when I grew up in Sudbury Tim Horton and I were good friends. Timmy wound up a great career in Buffalo and he was playing against the Leafs nursing a broken jaw. He was taking a lot of pills for it. He had a couple of drinks after the game and on his way back to Buffalo at four in the morning, Timmy was driving too fast and flew off the road. They'd even set up a road block trying to slow him down. His car flipped and he was killed. I learned from that that drinking and driving is wrong. So please be careful out there. Thank you.

Shack was never at a loss for words on the ice. One night at the Montreal Forum, after a scrap with the Pocket Rocket that earned them penalty time, he told the fuming Richard, "Henri, don't get so upset. It's not your fault that God gave all the hockey talent to your big brother."

Stump your friends with the following trivia. Name a player who scored 20 or more goals with five different NHL clubs. The answer is Eddie Shack. He scored 26 for the Leafs in 1965–66 — the year my brother-in-law (Bill McCauley) and I wrote the song about him — and more than 20 with the Bruins, Kings, Penguins, and Sabres later in his career.

Pulford Blasts Hayes

THREE players who would ultimately grace the Hockey Hall of Fame are the principals in the following anecdote. During a Montreal-Toronto game in the 1962–63 season, Bob Pulford, hard-working centreman for the Leafs, took a pass from a teammate and found himself skating in all alone on Montreal's Jacques Plante. Then he heard the blast of a whistle. Linesman George Hayes ruled that Pulford was offside and called for a faceoff outside the blueline. The crowd groaned and Pulford's face lit up like a Christmas tree. While he was lining up for the faceoff against the Habs' softspoken Jean Beliveau, he began questioning Hayes's eyesight.

"What the hell's wrong with you, George? Your eyes starting to fail you? You must have had three or four beers last night and you can't see straight."

Before Hayes could respond, Beliveau straightened up and said with a poker face. "Now that is a terrible insult to you, George." Then to Pulford he said, "You know he didn't drink three or four beers last night, Bob-bee. He drank the whole damn case!"

All three of them broke out in laughter.

Some time later, linesman Hayes, who had acquired a reputation over the years as the NHL's thirstiest linesman, was ordered to take an eye examination by league president Clarence Campbell. But the colourful official refused. He told reporters, "Anybody who can read the labels on the whiskey bottles from across the bar doesn't need an eye test."

Smythe Selected
Great Captains

IN many hockey organizations, the team captain is selected by a player vote. Leaf owner Conn Smythe wanted no part of a popularity contest or a secret ballot when an on-ice leader was needed. For as long as he governed the Leafs, he chose the captain. His last choice, before selling the club, was right winger George Armstrong.

"I picked George Armstrong because I want a man as captain who will give you everything he's got," Smythe told the media. "And he'll get the other players to do the same. Armstrong sets a great example, he's a gentleman all the way through and he is an outstanding leader, typifying everything that a Canadian should be. I've chosen some great captains over the years and George is one of the best of them."

When asked to comment on his other choices, Smythe replied,

Well, my captains have provided me with some of my fondest memories of my Maple Leaf teams. Hap Day was my captain in the early years and I don't think there was a more loyal, better captain. The players would follow him anywhere. Then we had Red Horner, and he was a great one, too — especially when the going got rough. Through the war years, we had Bob Davidson and I remember him playing in a Stanley Cup final where his check scored the winning goal. After the game he cried his eyes out because he blamed himself for the loss. With that same dedication he came back the next season to captain the Leafs to the Stanley Cup.

Then of course there was Syl Apps and Ted Kennedy. You couldn't invent a better captain than Apps if you wrote out the specifications. Then Teeder came along and did everything the others did and just as well. Charlie Conacher served a year as captain and so did Sid Smith — both good men.

One captain who infuriated Smythe was defenceman Jimmy Thomson. In 1957, Smythe discovered that Thomson was serving as vice-president of the newly-formed NHL Players' Association. Smythe hated the idea of a union for players and said as much.

> I don't want anyone telling us what we have to do. The way I see it, the Players' Association has not contributed a solitary thing to make hockey a better game. In fact, it's causing a good deal of trouble. I want our captain to be concerned with the Leafs and nothing else. When Thomson didn't see it my way, I traded him to the Blackhawks in a second. He would never have been my captain in the first place if I hadn't let Hap Day and the hockey committee influence me. I wanted George Armstrong and they chose Thomson. It was a bad choice but they can't blame that one on me.

George "Chief" Armstrong, the Native Son

In the days when racist barbs were common in sports, George Armstrong, captain of the Leafs, was often taunted from rinkside about his Indian heritage. He was, after all, half Ojibway and was an honorary Chief of the Stoney Tribe (named Big Chief Shoot-the-Puck).

During one game Armstrong heard one too many insults about his aboriginal roots. After the contest, he skated over and addressed the loudmouth fans.

"You guys aren't so smart. Think about this. When you white people came to this country the Indians knew how to run things. We paid no taxes. We had no debts. The women did most of the work and we menfolk spent all our time hunting and fishing. How can you beat a system like that?"

Armstrong combined great leadership with a captivating sense of humour. Johnny Bower, his roommate on road trips, was often the victim of an Armstrong prank. In the Leaf dressing room, Bower habitually placed his dentures in a small plastic cup before skating out for a game or practice. One day he returned to the room and popped in his teeth. But they failed to click into place. Frustrated, he pulled them out and examined them. That's when he realized they weren't his teeth. Somebody had substituted another set of false teeth during his absence. He looked across the room at Armstrong, who was trying to hold back his laughter.

"Damn you, Chief," fumed Bower. "You did this. Where'd you get these dentures — from a dentist?"

"No way," laughed Armstrong. "I got them from an undertaker."

It was Armstrong who scored the goal that wrapped up the last Toronto Stanley Cup triumph in 1967. Leading the Canadiens three games to two (Montreal rode the crest of a 15-game undefeated streak into the finals), and nursing a 2–1 lead into the final minute of play in game six, Armstrong scored into an empty net with 47 seconds left on the clock to assure a Toronto victory and the team's eleventh Stanley Cup.

He played 20 seasons in Toronto and scored 296 goals in 1,187 games. He was team captain for more than ten years, longer than any other Leaf captain. Throughout his career he was associated with champions. He played on a Memorial Cup winner, an Allan Cup winner, a Calder Cup winner (in Pittsburgh), and four Stanley Cup–winning teams. In 1975, Armstrong became the first native player to be inducted into the Hockey Hall of Fame.

A Raise?
You've Got to Be Kidding

IN the '60s, when the Leafs captured four Stanley Cups, their most difficult preseason challenge was garnering a satisfactory reward for their heroic efforts. Let's take Johnny Bower, the remarkable goalie who was often described by manager-coach Punch Imlach as "the greatest athlete in the world" as an example.

In 1964, after Bower had led the Leafs to the Cup, he told George Armstrong, his roommate, "I've got to see Punch about a raise."

Army asked, "How much is he paying you now?"

"Not much. Only $13,000."

"Geez," said Army, "that's a disgrace. You go in there and tell him you want a raise of $10,000. He knows the team can't win without you."

The next day before practice Bower met with Imlach and blurted out his request. Later he told Army, "I told Punch about the rising cost of living. I told him my wife is pregnant even though she's not. I told him I needed a new car."

"Yeah, and what did Imlach say?" asked Army.

"Imlach didn't say a word," replied Bower. "He just got up and opened the door and showed me the way out. Then he said, 'Bower, get out on that ice. And if you're so much as one minute late it's a $50 fine.'"

"What'd you do then?" asked the captain.

"Well, I ran for the dressing room," Bower said. "I didn't want to be late for practice and lose 50 bucks. That's a lot of money."

Over the next few days Bower had four more meetings with Imlach, and was thrown out of his office every time. During the fifth meeting, King Clancy sat in on the negotiations and urged Punch to loosen his purse strings — just a little.

"Punch said, 'Okay, I'll boost your salary by $2,500 but not a damn cent more.'"

"Is that all you got?" said Armstrong. "That's a joke."

"Aw, it's not so bad," replied Bower. "While I was in there I got thinking of all those years I spent riding those buses in the American League and how Punch might send me back there if I got him mad enough. I never want to ride those buses again."

Bower will never forget the Stanley Cup victory in 1964. He recorded a 4–0 shutout over Detroit in the seventh game of the finals and then threw his goal stick high in the air to celebrate the great triumph. Trouble is, he forgot to follow its flight. His stick crashed down on his head and cut him for six stitches.

Bower the Penny Pincher

T HE Leafs of the '60s used to kid goalie Johnny Bower about his frugal ways. One of them told me how Bower financed a new suit for himself at the end of each season.

> You see, John was one of our cab captains. That meant Imlach would dole out a few bucks for cab fare. Four or five players would share a cab to and from the arena and the cab captain would pay. Believe me, there was often nothing left over for a tip because Imlach had those costs figured to the dime.
>
> But Bower's figuring was even better because he always found a way to come out of that cab with a few coins left over. And these he saved. By the end of the year, he'd saved enough to visit Mickey Allen's in Montreal and buy himself a new suit. It happened every year.

Bower might not have had to be so frugal if Imlach had paid him what he was worth. Anyone who saw him play would place Bower on any all-time Leaf All-Star team.

Sawchuk's
Magnificent Stand

IT was one of the greatest goaltending performances I've ever seen. And it took place on April 15, 1967.

Bill Hewitt and I were in the broadcast booth at the old Chicago Stadium covering the Toronto-Chicago Stanley Cup semifinal series, which was tied at two games apiece. I remember thinking how fortunate the Leafs were to be involved in a fifth game. Chicago had dominated throughout the regular season, finishing 19 points ahead of fourth-place Toronto and outscoring the Leafs by 60 goals.

But strong goaltending can make up for other deficiencies and the Leafs were getting it from veteran Terry Sawchuk in the two-thirds of a game he was asked to play.

He hadn't wanted to be in goal that afternoon. He'd played all four games of the series. His back was sore and his body was battered and bruised. He pleaded with Punch Imlach for a break, so Imlach gave Johnny Bower the job of stopping Bobby Hull, Stan Mikita, and the rest of the Hawks.

But the layoff had affected Bower. His timing was off and he began juggling pucks. At the end of the first period, Imlach looked at the scarred face of Sawchuk and nodded. Sawchuk sighed and nodded back. He was ready.

Early in the second period Bobby Hull drove the puck with such force that it almost embedded itself in Sawchuk's shoulder. Sawchuk collapsed in a heap and Bob Haggert, the Leaf trainer, rushed out on the ice.

"Are you okay, Uke? Are you okay?"

Sawchuk moaned, then snapped, "I stopped the damn thing, didn't I? Now help me up."

He hobbled back into his net and finished the game in glorious fashion, slamming the door on the Blackhawk sharpshooters in a display of goaltending that was simply awesome. He stopped 37 shots, 22 in the final period. Pete Stemkowski scored the winning goal in the third period and Jim Pappin added an insurance marker as the Leafs won 4–2.

Sawchuk was magnificent again in game six at Maple Leaf Gardens and the Leafs advanced against Montreal with a 3–1 victory.

Spoiling Montreal's Planned Party

I**T** was Centennial Year — 1967 — and the Montreal Canadiens planned to celebrate the momentous occasion with a Stanley Cup triumph. Lord Stanley's old silverware and Expo, both in Montreal.

The Toronto Maple Leafs appeared to have an empty tank when they faced rookie goalie Rogatien Vachon and the Habs at the Forum. "Don't tell me they're starting some Junior B goalie against us," squawked Imlach. Game one was a slaughter, a 6–2 Hab victory. Mrs. Imlach, watching on TV, got so angry with the Toronto telecast crew's description of the shellacking that she was tempted to kick in her TV set. Good thing Bill Hewitt and I didn't run into her in the next couple of days.

The Toronto writers were much more caustic. One said it was like a battle between jet fighters and Sopwith Camels. Vachon said, "Maybe Punch will call me a Junior A goalie now." Terry Sawchuk had been banged up in the opener so Johnny Bower started in game two. Amazingly, he shut out the Habs 3–0 and showed great poise, even though he was belted three times by John Ferguson, who stampeded through his crease like an angry buffalo.

Back in Toronto for game three, Bower ignored his swollen nose (whacked by Ferguson's stick) and stopped 60 shots in a game that went into sudden-death overtime. The overtime was packed with thrills, drama, pressure, and close calls. Finally Bob Pulford slipped the gamewinner behind Gump Worsley at 28 minutes, 26 seconds of extra time.

Bower drew the starting assignment in game four but a pulled muscle in the warm-up sent him limping off and Sawchuk was forced to come in cold. But the old warrior played poorly and once again gave up six goals in a 6–2 loss.

For the second time in the series, Leaf fans and members of the media tumbled off the bandwagon. Critics declared the Leafs all finished, game old codgers but shooters of last bolts.

Bower, it turned out, was through for the year and Sawchuk looked like a survivor of the Springhill mine disaster. The Habs couldn't wait to start peppering the man they'd beaten ten times in two games.

But Sawchuk, who'd recorded his 100th career shutout earlier in the year, played near-perfect hockey in game five. He allowed just one goal — a deflection — and skated off with a 4–1 victory.

For game six Imlach dressed Bower as backup even though he could barely walk. Imlach didn't plan to use him (he had Al Smith half dressed, waiting in the Leaf dressing room) but he wanted Bower to share in the glory if the Leafs won. He was also thinking of the expansion draft, and how it would rob his team of many of his favourite players. It was the end of an era for his Leafs and he was determined it would end with memories that would last a lifetime. He even wore a new green-checked suit that night, one he'd purchased in Montreal after the humiliating defeat in game one. He'd told Tony the tailor, "I'll be wearing this suit on the night we win the Cup. You watch for it on TV." Tony had laughed at Imlach's optimism.

Once more Sawchuk reached back and found a way to match some of his best playoff performances from the past. Ellis and Pappin scored for the Leafs and Dick Duff was the Hab who spoiled his shutout bid.

The game came down to the final minute of play. There was a faceoff to the left of Sawchuk in the Leaf zone. Imlach surprised everyone by sending out his oldtimers in this crucial situation. There was Allan Stanley, Tim Horton, George Armstrong, Red Kelly, and Bob Pulford in front of Sawchuk. Stanley was told to take the faceoff against Beliveau. "Great," said the defenceman, "I can't remember when I last took a faceoff. And the way I take them is illegal."

The puck was dropped and Stanley stepped into Beliveau and held his stick. The puck went to Kelly, who moved it up to Pulford. Pulford sent a perfect cross-ice pass to Armstrong, who was moving up the right boards. The Leaf captain, from long range, calmly drilled the puck into the empty Montreal net to guarantee the victory. Meanwhile Beliveau was screaming "faceoff interference" at the referee. But the crowd noise created by thousands of jubilant fans drowned out his words. Beliveau shrugged and conceded defeat. The Leafs had captured the Stanley Cup and spoiled the Habs' plans for a centennial celebration of their own, with Expo the site of their grand soiree.

Moving the Big M

IN 1968 it was obvious to all that the Big M and the Big I were on a collision course. Frank Mahovlich and Punch Imlach were barely speaking and Imlach — very secretly — made plans to get rid of the moody Mahovlich, even though the big left winger's dazzling rushes and goal production had made him a favourite with most Leaf fans.

The fans, of course, never knew that Imlach offered Mahovlich even up for Stan Mikita of Chicago. Nor did they know that he talked with Montreal and offered to take an aging (37) Jean Beliveau in return for Mahovlich.

When nothing developed from one-for-one proposals, Imlach thought in terms of a multi-player swap, and the player he began with was former star defenceman Carl Brewer. The Red Wings had shown some interest in Brewer, who'd walked out on Imlach in 1965. But the Leafs still owned Brewer's NHL rights.

"Would the Wings be interested in Brewer and Mahovlich?" Imlach asked Sid Abel, his counterpart in Detroit.

"You bet," said Abel. "But what do we give up in return?"

"How about sending us Norm Ullman and Paul Henderson?"

"Well, we're not sure Brewer will play for us," said Abel. "And Ullman's a proven star. Sweeten the pot a bit. Give us Mike Walton and that promising kid you've got — Gary Unger. And we'll throw Floyd Smith into our end of the deal."

"No, Walton's my top scorer," replied Imlach. "And Unger shows a lot of promise. Let me think about it."

Both men mulled over the names they'd discussed.

Then Abel called. "If I can't get Walton, I'll take Stemkowski," he told Imlach. "But Unger has to be included."

It was a deal. The agreement was made on Friday, March 1, 1968. Ullman, Henderson, and Smith to the Leafs in exchange for Mahovlich, Stemkowski, Unger, and the rights to Brewer. Abel and Imlach both stressed the importance of keeping the swap a secret until all the players involved could be notified. Both clubs would announce the trade simultaneously on Monday morning at 11 a.m.

But over the weekend, someone in the Leaf organization leaked the information to the media. It might have been Harold Ballard, who had to be told about the trade and expressed concern about dealing Mahovlich. It could have been Stafford Smythe. Or one of the Leaf directors, who had to give their approval. "Why the hell the directors had to be consulted was beyond me," Imlach said later. "It was ridiculous. Some of those guys didn't go to see 30 games a year."

The names of the players involved were in all the papers. Mahovlich and the others got calls early Monday morning from people asking them if it was true they'd been traded.

Imlach was livid over the leak and called Abel. "Look, some ass in our executive suite leaked the news and I promised you it wouldn't happen. Now if you want to cancel the trade, I'm giving you that option." Abel thought it over for a few seconds and said, "No, Punch, the trade is a go."

Under Imlach, Mahovlich had suffered two bouts of "nervous exhaustion and depression" and had been hospitalized. If he'd remained with the Leafs and Imlach, chances are he'd have retired early — at least ten years prematurely.

In Detroit he scored a career-high 49 goals in 1968–69 and combined with Alex Delvecchio and Gordie Howe for 118 goals, a new mark for line scoring. In 1971 he was traded to Montreal and played superbly there until 1974. He finished his career in the WHA with the Toronto Toros and the Birmingham Bulls, retiring in 1978.

Despite the Big M's inability to get along with the Big I in Toronto, Imlach had kind words for the superstar in his book, *Hockey Is a Battle*. He wrote: "He's got a damn good head on his shoulders and he's a pretty level-headed guy. He just wanted to be left alone; at least that's what it seemed to me. He is one of the most high-class individuals, one of the finest guys, you'd ever want to meet."

Those of us who've been privileged to know the Big M over the years would heartily agree.

Mahovlich was an instant star in the NHL, winning the Calder Trophy over Bobby Hull in his first season. He played on six Stanley Cup winners with Toronto and Montreal and finished his career with 533 goals and 1,103 points. He was inducted into the Hockey Hall of Fame in 1981.

Nailing a Superstar

THERE we were, Bill Hewitt and myself, in our cramped broadcast location at the Boston Garden on April 2, 1969, for the opening game of the Stanley Cup semifinals between the Boston Bruins and the Toronto Maple Leafs. The Bruins were a rising superpower in the game, with stars like Esposito, Bucyk, Cashman, Hodge, and the wondrous Bobby Orr, then in his third NHL campaign. On many a night Orr was virtually unstoppable. On this night he was stopped cold by a brash rookie — Patrick Quinn.

The game itself was a stinker, with the Bruins romping to a 10–0 triumph. But what Quinn did to Orr almost triggered a riot in the stands and in the penalty box.

In the second period Orr grabbed the puck and started to break out of his own zone on the right side. Suddenly, there was Quinn, cruising in from the blue line. For a split second Orr glanced down at the puck and WHAM! Quinn nailed him. Orr staggered back and collapsed to the ice from the hardest check he'd ever received. Quinn stood over him, as if to say, I can't believe I hit the guy.

Referee John Ashley skated over and signalled a penalty to Quinn. Five minutes for elbowing. In the broadcast booth I remember saying to Hewitt, "It might have been charging but all in all, it looked like a pretty good check. Orr just wasn't expecting it."

All hell broke loose throughout the building while Orr lay there unconscious. The trainers rushed out to examine him. Quinn skated reluctantly to the penalty box, where a hundred maniacal fans waited for him. They threw punches at him and pelted him with programs. For his own safety he was urged to escape to the Leaf dressing room.

Meanwhile Orr was taken to hospital where doctors treated him for a slight concussion. Quinn's check might have been the most devastating one he ever received but did it slow him down? Not much. The following season he created history by becoming the first defenceman to lead the NHL in scoring, with 120 points.

As for Quinn, he has become much more renowned in the game's front office than he ever was on the ice. But looking back, he calls his check on Orr "my most memorable moment as a defenceman."

Bobby Orr and Wayne Gretzky top my personal list of the most amazing hockey players I have seen. Orr won the Norris Trophy eight straight times and in 1970 he became the first NHLer to capture four individual trophies in a single season: the Norris as top defenceman, the Art Ross Trophy as scoring leader, the Hart Trophy as league MVP, and the Conn Smythe Trophy as playoff MVP.

Forbes Kennedy's
Last NHL Game

I**T'S** ironic that two incidents in one playoff game — a game that was predictable almost from the opening faceoff — would stand tall in one's memory over a quarter of a century later. Both occurred in the Toronto-Boston playoff game on April 2, 1969, a 10–0 romp for the Bruins.

I have already cited Pat Quinn's thumping check that concussed Bobby Orr that night and sent him glassy-eyed to the hospital.

When the game continued, another Leaf newcomer, Forbes Kennedy, threw his last punch in the NHL and ended his career with a pageful of penalties. Kennedy challenged every Bruin in his path that night and during one brawl he threw a punch that bowled over George Ashley, the linesman.

I said to Bill Hewitt, my broadcast partner, "Now Kennedy's in real trouble. That punch will be reported to NHL headquarters and Kennedy faces a stiff fine and a probable suspension." Subsequently Kennedy was fined $1,000 and suspended for four games. The April 2 game was his last in the league. (The Leafs lost the next three games and were eliminated and Kennedy did not return the following season.)

Back in Toronto for games three and four, I was told by King Clancy that Punch Imlach was furious with me. "Punch says you're the guy that got Kennedy suspended and he's really pissed off. He says he watched the tapes and Kennedy never hit the guy. Imlach wants to see you." I said, "King, I don't work for Punch. I work for *Hockey Night in Canada*. If he wants to talk to me, tell him to call me."

Punch never called and I avoided him for the next couple of days, figuring he might cool off. After the fourth game at the Gardens (and fourth straight win for the Bruins), the Toronto season was all over. Driving home after the game that night, I heard on the radio, "Punch Imlach has just been fired by Stafford Smythe."

I turned to my wife and said, "I guess that's good news. If Smythe hadn't fired Punch, I'm pretty sure Punch was going to try and have me fired."

For a quarter of a century I harboured a nagging doubt. What if Punch was right and Kennedy hadn't slugged the linesman that night? Two summers ago I ran into Kennedy at a golf tournament in Sydney, Nova Scotia. "All right, Forbes, tell me the truth. Did you punch George Ashley, the linesman, that night in Boston?" He laughed and said, "Oh, yeah. I whacked him a good one."

———————

One more note from the Official NHL Guide and Record Book, under Individual Playoff Records:

Most Penalties, One Playoff Game:
     8 — Forbes Kennedy, Toronto, April 2, 1969, at Boston. Four minors, 2 majors, 1 ten-minute misconduct, 1 game misconduct. Final score: Boston 10, Toronto 0.

It may have been his final game but he set a few records before he waved goodbye.

British Fan Witnesses First Game — And It's a Pip

IMAGINE seeing your first hockey game and it turns out to be one of the most memorable games ever played. That's what happened when reporter Ron Begley of the London, England, *Daily Mirror* visited Maple Leaf Gardens for the final game of the 1967 playoffs.

The following day he wrote:

I came 3,000 miles from Britain to see my first NHL game — and what a magnificent evening it was at Maple Leaf Gardens. The Leafs' Stanley Cup triumph was one of the most dramatic and exciting sporting victories I have seen, and that comes from a scribe who has been brought up on F.A. Cup finals at Wembley, the Grand National, the British Open Golf Championship, etc.

Last night's battle was the first BIG game I have seen and please don't ask me to quote the rules. But ask me about the pace of the game and I'll say "terrific." Ask me about the atmosphere created by a packed house of hockey fans and I'll say "exciting." And ask me about Terry Sawchuk and I will tell you he is marvellous.

I know that veteran skipper George Armstrong's goal in the final minute sent tears of delight rolling down the cheeks of many Toronto fans. I'm told it could be the "oldtimer's" last shot in hockey.

But it was Sawchuk who laid the foundation of the Leafs' victory. I did not imagine that such a heavily-padded man on skates could put up such a brilliantly mobile performance.

Sawchuk was never out of position in the opening period, when, to my inexperienced eyes, Canadiens threatened to run away with the match. He brought off saves that reminded me of the finest soccer goal keepers of the world.

And when Canadiens roared back in the game last night, cutting the Leafs' edge to 2–1, it was Sawchuk again who gave his team the will to win. But let's not forget Canadiens. They sprang from defence to attack much quicker than the Leafs.

At least, that is how things appeared to my eyes, which are used to the somewhat leisurely game of soccer. And they almost popped out at some of the tough stuff which would have brought hordes of screaming soccer fans racing onto the pitch back home.

Dorey's Debut

I WAS talking with Jim Dorey recently about a night we both remember vividly, his first game at Maple Leaf Gardens. It was a game between the Leafs and the Pittsburgh Penguins. On October 16, 1968, 16,321 fans showed up to see Punch Imlach's new-look Leafs open the season with a 2–2 tie against the visitors. They went home talking about the Leafs' kid defenceman, Jim Dorey.

One wild, second-period brawl put Dorey, a Kingston lad, into the NHL record book. After attacking Ken Schinkel, Keith McCreary, and John Arbour physically and referee Art Skov verbally, Dorey was finally banished to the Leaf dressing room as the league's all-time worst single-game offender.

His eight penalties — four minors, two majors, a misconduct, and a game misconduct — established an individual record (the old mark was seven, held by George Boucher of Ottawa and Ted Green of Boston) and his total of 48 minutes was one more than that amassed one night by Chicago's renowned scrapper Reggie Fleming.

In addition Dorey drew automatic fines totalling $125.

After he was tossed, Dorey barged into the dressing room and left the rink without comment.

Dorey told me,

> I couldn't believe what I'd done. I sat in the dressing room with my head down, thinking of how far down in the minors Punch would send me. I wondered if my career was all over after just one game, and then I heard footsteps approaching. I looked up and King Clancy was there. He said, "That's the kind of spirit we like to see, Jimmy-boy." And he slapped me on the back. Then Imlach was there and he pulled out his wallet. "Here's a hundred bucks, kid. Get the hell out of here before the reporters come in. Take the weekend off and forget all about what happened tonight."
>
> And that's what I did. If Punch had chewed me out or made me feel stupid I might have quit hockey on the spot.

While Dorey's penalty-minute record set tongues wagging at the time (one writer compared him to Attila the Hun), other hard-nosed players' deeds have erased his sins from the book. Pittsburgh's Russ Anderson once collected 51 penalty minutes in a game, Philadelphia's Frank Bathe compiled 55 penalty minutes in a 1979 game against Los Angeles, and in the same match the Kings' Randy Holt was assessed one minor, three majors, two 10-minute misconducts, and three game misconducts, for a grand total of 67 minutes. By comparison, Holt makes Dorey look like a choir boy.

Dorey Launches Missile, Downs Golden Jet

AT the Chicago Stadium one night, Jim Dorey headed for the Leaf bench after finishing a tough shift. He was catching his breath when he noticed Bobby Hull, the Hawks' Golden Jet, starting to wind up with the puck. Hull flew past Ronnie Ellis and found himself in the clear. Impulsively, Dorey grabbed the plastic water bottle next to him and hurled it at the Hawk star. Direct hit! The bottle struck Hull on the side of the head and down he went.

The referee signalled a penalty but Dorey, by then, was bending down pretending to tie a skate lace. Leaf coach John McLellan shouted down the bench, "Whoever threw that bottle, get in the penalty box!" Rickey Ley, sitting next to Dorey, shouted back, "What did you say, coach?" And the crowd figured Ley for the bottle-tosser.

Finally, the referee ordered Dorey to the penalty box. En route he passed the fuming Hull. Dorey gave Hull an innocent look and said, "Bobby, it wasn't me who threw the damn bottle. It was Rickey Ley."

Dorey said, "Hull and Ley had some great mixups over the years and I think it all started with that water bottle incident. Finally, at a banquet in Kingston a few years ago, I told Bobby the truth. He got a big laugh out of it."

––––––––––––––

Jim Dorey played for the Leafs from 1968–69 to 1971–72, when he was traded to the Rangers. He was with the Rangers for a brief time when the New England Whalers of the WHA made him an offer he couldn't believe and couldn't refuse. He says, "By leaving New York I forced Ranger manager Emile Francis to more than double the salaries of his star players — men like Rod Gilbert, Jean Ratelle, and Vic Hadfield. Their salaries jumped from about 60 grand a year to 250 grand a year. Francis feared his best Rangers would follow my lead and jump to the WHA."

One More Story from Jim Dorey

WHEN I was with the Toros, Evel Knievel came to town. Remember him, the famous stuntman? Once rode a motorcycle over the Snake River Canyon. Or tried to. Broke more bones in his day than all the NHLers put together. Anyway, owner John Bassett of the Toros brought him in for a special between-periods promotion. The famous daredevil could earn $5,000 a goal if he could score on one of our Toros' netminders.

Nobody thought he could, of course, but Bassett was no fool. He knew that Larry Mavety and I knew our way around town, so he gave us his gold Visa card and set us up with a big limousine. And he told us, "Lookit, I want you to entertain this Knievel guy. He likes the nightlife, so I want you two to wear him right out. Just make sure he'll be so hung over he won't even be able to lace on a pair of skates by tomorrow afternoon."

Talk about nice assignments. That night we went to every gin mill in town and ordered drinks till they were coming out our ears. Old Evel kept pace with us all night. Finally we rolled him back to his hotel at about 5:30 in the morning, and guess what — he insisted we come up for a nightcap!

God, we were in rough shape the next day. And we're playing Gordie Howe and Houston Aeros. I didn't think we'd ever make it to the first intermission to watch our pal Knievel. The deal was $5,000 for each goal. Evel would have four attempts. Johnny Bassett was a little concerned, so he yanked Gilles Gratton, our young netminder, and replaced him with the more experienced Les Binkley.

Evel skated out wearing number 13. He told us earlier he hadn't skated in 13 years. He acknowledged the roar of the crowd, grabbed that puck, and scored on Binkley. Then, by God, he did it again! He went two for four. We couldn't believe it. The guy looked like he'd just had 12 hours sleep. Then we found out he'd played some pretty competitive hockey out west somewhere. Junior B or A maybe. Anyway, he collected $10,000 bucks in about 20 seconds.

Bassett came around later and he was fuming. "I thought I told you guys to take care of him last night," he said.

"Boss, we did," I protested. "We kept the son of a bitch up all night. But he drank us under the table. We couldn't have done anything more unless we'd poisoned him."

Ballard and Obodiac

IN 1968 I went to work for Harold Ballard. After I sent him a plan outlining how the image of the Gardens could be enhanced, he offered me the job of publicity director. I was shocked at how little he was willing to pay for such a position: $8,500 per annum. I said I'd take the position providing I could have some free time to write books and freelance on radio. He said he didn't give a damn what I did in my free time.

During my first day on the job, he came to me and said, "You know, you've already caused me a problem. Stan Obodiac is pissed off because I hired you. He thinks he's my publicity director and he's been with me a long time so I'll have to find you another title." But I can't recall whether he ever did or not.

After nine months on the job, it was over. Ballard didn't want to spend any money implementing any of my plans, and I had had enough of Ballard and the Gardens. One day, on the eve of my summer vacation, one of Harold's flunkeys came around and mumbled something about Ballard wanting to close down the publicity department. That was enough of a hint for me. The job was going nowhere anyway. So, without ever speaking to Ballard, I went on vacation and never went back.

But Stan Obodiac survived Ballard's tempestuous and penny-pinching nature for another 17 years. Obodiac was always fiercely loyal to the Gardens and his controversial boss, despite the mere pittance he received for a job that demanded his attention seven days a week. In 1984, after 26 years of service, Obodiac was earning just over $23,000. Four years earlier he had earned $18,000. Rival teams in the NHL were paying their publicity men between $50,000 and $60,000 a year for similar chores. None of them were putting in the hours required of Obodiac.

But Obodiac never complained. He lauded Ballard as a "great humanitarian and philanthropist." He wrote dozens of letters to the newspapers, extolling Ballard's many virtues.

And he was ready at all times to obey Ballard's every command. If Ballard promised a friend an autograph of a Leaf player, he thought nothing of phoning Obodiac at home, interrupting him at the dinner table, and ordering him to find the player and get his signature on paper. Obodiac would leave his meal, jump into his car, and fulfill the request. Fortunately, he possessed a company car, one of the few perks in his profession.

In 1985, Stan Obodiac died of liver cancer. Before he passed away, Ballard asked him to drop the ceremonial puck prior to the Leaf home opener in 1984. Obodiac was thrilled at the honour.

Later, Ballard gave Obodiac an airline ticket to Hawaii. Ballard often presented his players (and their wives) with airline tickets as Christmas presents. It was suspected that he received a batch of tickets in a contra arrangement with the airlines involved and paid virtually nothing for the ducats. In Obodiac's case it was a single ticket. Unlike the players' wives, his wife, Emma, was ignored. Because the Obodiacs had no funds to purchase an extra ticket to Hawaii, Emma encouraged Stan to go by himself. He did, but he was quite sick and very lonely and did not enjoy the trip.

On the eve of his death in the spring of 1985, Obodiac phoned Ballard and told him what a great man he was and how much Obodiac appreciated all that the Leaf owner had done for him.

At the funeral later that week, Ballard did not approach Obodiac's widow or his children. The following day Emma Obodiac was awakened early in the morning by a Ballard employee hammering on her door. He was there to collect the company car. "I thought they might have phoned me first," she said bitterly. "I knew I wouldn't be able to keep the car.

"I was further shocked to learn that Stan's pension was a mere $277.06 per month," continued Mrs. Obodiac. "Two years earlier, Stan had been forced to ask Mr. Ballard for an advance on his salary because we simply couldn't pay our bills." She added, "To this day Mr. Ballard has not called or written a note to express his appreciation for the 26 years of devoted service Stan gave to him and the Gardens."

When Toronto *Globe* sportswriter William Houston asked Mrs. Obodiac why Stan put up with the working conditions under Ballard, she said, "Stan loved his job there and considered it an honour to work at Maple Leaf Gardens."

And when Houston reached Ballard by telephone and asked him to comment on his treatment of a devoted employee, Ballard refused to comment. He snarled, "Just keep writing the bullshit you usually write. What do I care?"

6

THE SEVENTIES

The Death of a Legend

WHEN Marcel Pronovost walked into his son's room on that day in 1970, little Leo was sobbing. The eight-year-old held Terry Sawchuk's goaltending glove in his hands and tears spilled into the pocket. He'd just heard the news: Terry Sawchuk was dead.

"Terry was Leo's idol," said Pronovost, a catch in his voice. "And I'm just as shocked and saddened with the news of his death. He was such a great fellow. He was my friend and my roommate. We were very close."

The cause of Sawchuk's death a quarter of a century ago remains something of a mystery. On the night of April 29, 1970, Sawchuk and his New York Ranger teammate Ron Stewart were living in a rented home in Long Beach, on the ocean side of Long Island.

Stewart was seen at the E and J Pub on nearby West Beach that evening. After having a few drinks, he was just leaving when Sawchuk came in. Something happened to Sawchuk in the next few hours, something outside the bar, an incident that required Sawchuk's hospitalization and two major operations. It was said that he argued with Stewart, that the two men scuffled and Sawchuk was grievously injured when he fell on a drain pipe or a barbecue or some other obstacle. Stewart refused to comment.

Sawchuk was rushed to hospital, where he had his gall bladder removed. A few days later he required a second operation. He died of cardiac arrest following the procedure.

Sawchuk, at age 40, was no stranger to hospitals. During his playing career, during which he compiled a record 103 shutouts, he suffered such medical infirmities as herniated discs, a gashed eye, severed wrist tendons, mononucleosis, arthritis, a collapsed lung (in an auto accident), bone chips in the elbow and a deformed elbow, spinal fusion, and a swayback condition caused from constant bending at the waist.

NHL president Clarence Campbell said, "It was a ghastly tragedy, which left seven children fatherless." Sawchuk was survived by his ex-wife, Patricia (they divorced a year earlier), and their children.

New York Ranger general manager Emile Francis said Sawchuk's passing was a shocking loss to hockey. "He was one of the greatest goaltenders of all time. For the record, he was seven times an All-Star and winner of the Vezina Trophy four times. One year in eight playoff games he had four shutouts and his goals-against average was an unbelievable 0.62. He was rookie-of-the-year in every league he played in; with Omaha of the USHL in 1948, with Indianapolis of the AHL a year later, and with the Detroit Red Wings in 1951."

Paul Dulmage, writing in the old Toronto *Telegram*, recalled how Sawchuk signed his first pro contract with Jack Adams of Detroit. "He took the $2,000 cheque, cashed it and took the money home. Then he threw the bills in the air and danced under them in glee. He was 17 years old. Ahead of him lay 23 years of fame, fortune, pain and heartbreak."

Sawchuk often said his finest moment was leading the Leafs to their last Stanley Cup — the stunning upset of Montreal in 1967.

Plante Tutors Parent

H E was an old man of 41 when he joined the Leafs in May, 1970. A goaltending legend, Jacques Plante had won seven Vezina trophies in the old six-team NHL and captured another (shared with Glenn Hall) when he was coaxed out of retirement to play with the expansion St. Louis Blues in 1968. Two seasons later the Blues no longer needed the man who made the goal mask a fixture in hockey, so they sold him to Toronto where he shared the netminding duties with Bernie Parent. And what a season he turned in for the Leafs! Plante allowed just 73 goals in 40 games, for an astonishing 1.88 goals-against average. Once before, playing with a powerhouse Montreal team in 1955–56, he recorded a slightly better average — 1.86.

But he was not the most popular Leaf in the dressing room or on the ice. Defenceman Jim McKenny recalls Plante's temper tantrums. "If a defenceman screened him on a shot and the puck went in, and I was guilty of that from time to time, he'd point the glove and scream and shout at you. It was embarrassing. I figured the best thing to do when Plante was scored on was to get the hell off the ice. Beat it to the bench before Plante, and the TV cameras, would show the nation what a numbskull you were."

One Leaf of that era who idolized Plante was fellow netminder Bernie Parent. Parent credited the veteran stopper with teaching him the fine points of goaltending. But their association with the Leafs was a brief one. At the end of the 1973 season, Plante was traded to Boston for Eddie Johnston and a draft choice (Ian Turnbull). Parent, for some reason, disliked living in Toronto and in 1972 jumped to a team that never really existed, the WHA's Miami Screaming Eagles. In time he landed back in the NHL with the Philadelphia Flyers, where the lessons taught by Plante, his mentor, paid off. Parent won back-to-back Conn Smythe trophies as the Flyers captured consecutive Stanley Cups in 1974 and 1975. His brilliant career ended prematurely during the 1978–79 season when a stick wielded by a Ranger player penetrated a small hole in his mask and damaged his eye. His sight was saved but he was forced to retire.

Glennie Versus Mikita: Memories of Moscow

BRIAN Glennie played 10 years in the NHL, joining the Leafs in 1969. By 1972 he was a member of Team Canada, used sparingly in that memorable eight-game series with the Soviets that culminated in Paul Henderson's winning goal in the final few seconds of play in Moscow.

Last summer, at our annual NHL Oldtimer's get-together in Markham, Ontario, the committee recruited Glennie as a speaker and he wowed us with the following tale:

> Stan Mikita and I were spare bodies during that series in '72 and in Moscow we tried to keep in shape with some extra practice between games. We were doing some one-on-ones this day, and Mikita, looking a little the worse for wear — he'd obviously been heavily into the vodka the night before — came down on me, stopped, and barfed all over the ice. I leaped back as Mikita pulled himself together, waltzed in, and scored.
>
> Now it's a couple of months later and I'm back with the Leafs and we're playing Chicago. Who comes sailing down the ice against me but my old pal Mikita. I'm the only Leaf back and I'm giving him plenty of room because he was deadly when he got in close on a defenceman. Suddenly he stops in front of me and drills a slapshot into our net. When he saw the surprised look on my face he laughed and said, "What's the matter, big guy? Think I was going to puke on you again?"

Pyramid Power

WHEN Red Kelly coached the Leafs, he was always searching for a playoff gimmick that would help his Leafs surmount some very large obstacles — like the Philadelphia Flyers for instance. In 1976, Red introduced pyramid power to pro hockey. Kelly had heard about the mystical powers of pyramids and he ordered a large one hung from the ceiling in the Leaf dressing room. Smaller ones were situated under the players' bench. If players spent time under the pyramid, or even placed their sticks under it, he told his men, good things were bound to happen. Of course they were skeptical, but they were also superstitious and when team captain Darryl Sittler tried it, he went out and scored five goals against the Flyers in an 8–5 Toronto rout.

Those were the days when the Flyers' good-luck charm was a doddering singer, Kate Smith by name. When Kate sang "God Bless America" before home games, the Flyers invariably won. Asked to compare the respective good-luck charms of the two teams, Tiger Williams said, "I'd rather be sitting under a pyramid in our room than sitting under Kate Smith in theirs."

The Leafs were eliminated in the seventh game and Kelly disposed of his pyramids — forever.

But he was a willing convert to other concepts never seen in hockey. One year he was convinced that positive and negative ions had much to do with a team's winning record. And the Leafs jumped on the ion bandwagon. Another time he was told that bright colours could not only drive gloom from a room but could lead to a positive attitude. He promptly had his team's dressing room repainted in bright tones and ordered the visiting team's room to be repainted in the dullest possible colours.

While coaching Pittsburgh one season, he decided to block the deafening crowd noise in the St. Louis Arena by issuing earmuffs to his players. Even the coach donned the headwear. All went well for the first few seconds. Then the Blues scored and off came all the muffs. "That ended that," said Kelly. "You couldn't hear yourself think in there, with or without the earmuffs."

Kelly, incidentally, was renowned as a hockey man who never swore. One night while coaching the Leafs, he exploded in anger and uttered a four-letter word. "Darn it, you fellows aren't playing worth *hell!*" he shouted.

Mouths popped open. Eyes took on a glassy look. The Leafs had never heard their coach use such profanity.

It was Jim McKenny who broke the silence. "Red, I know we're screwing up out there but you don't have to swear at us like that."

Kelly enjoyed a fabulous career as defenceman, forward, and coach. He scored 281 career goals and sipped champagne from the Stanley Cup eight times, four with Detroit and four more with the Leafs. He leads all non–Montreal Canadiens in Cup victories. He served two terms in Parliament while playing for the Leafs but his arduous schedule never seemed to hamper his play. The first season Frank Mahovlich played left wing to Kelly's centre, the Big M's goal production went from 18 to 48.

Sittler's Record Still Stands

IN all the thousands of NHL games that have been played, it happened only once. How fortunate I was to be at Maple Leaf Gardens on the night of February 7, 1976, to help describe the feat on *Hockey Night in Canada*. It was the most amazing individual performance, from a scoring standpoint, in NHL history. It was Darryl Sittler's 10-point night against the Boston Bruins.

It's coming on 20 years since Sittler went on his point-collecting spree against a porous rookie netminder in the Boston goal. Dave Reece was just a kid, a rookie out of college hockey seeking steady employment in the NHL. Looking back, Sittler says of his six goals and four assists for ten points, "As much as the fans fault Reece for what happened, it was simply a night where every shot and pass I made seemed to pay off in a goal. I hit the corners a couple of times, banking shots in off the post. The kid was screened on a couple of goals and had no chance. He didn't really flub one goal. On the tenth point I banked a shot in from behind the net off Brad Park's leg."

As Sittler's points totals mounted that night, in the broadcast booth Bill Hewitt and I, during commercial breaks, were kept busy looking up past records. Montreal's Maurice Richard had scored eight points in a game in 1944. Ten years later the Habs' Bert Olmstead had matched that total in a 12–1 rout of Chicago. Sittler scored hat tricks in consecutive periods — a feat never before accomplished. He tied another mark with five points in the second period.

Since that night of high drama at the Gardens, the closest anyone has come to matching Sittler's record is eight points in a game. Wayne Gretzky and Mario Lemieux have done it twice. The other eight-point scorers are Tom Bladon, Bryan Trottier, Peter Stastny, Anton Stastny, Paul Coffey, and Bernie Nicholls.

Because hockey is such an unpredictable game, Sittler's mark may be shattered next week, it may last another 20 years, or it may be around for ever. The last is most likely, for it took 13,500 games for the first 10-point night. If Wayne and Mario weren't able to match it at the peak of their scoring prowess, who among the current crop of snipers is a candidate to match the Sittler mark? Sittler says, "It's one of the few scoring records that Wayne Gretzky hasn't broken. And when you think about it, there aren't that many times a team will score ten goals in a game. And how long are the odds for a player to figure in every one of them?"

It wasn't as if a hot-handed Sittler was feasting off a mediocre club that February night in '76. The Bruins, coached by Don Cherry, had rolled into Toronto riding a seven-game winning streak. Ironically, that week Sittler had been publicly scolded by cantankerous Leaf owner Harold Ballard for a scoring drought during which he'd scored only one goal in his past eight games.

It was Sittler's most memorable season in the NHL. He followed up his 10-point night with a five-goal performance against Philadelphia in a playoff game to tie another record, and that fall he slapped in the overtime winner against Czechoslovakia in the deciding game of the first Canada Cup series.

———————

Sittler would later fall from favour with Leaf management and become involved in a bitter dispute with general manager Punch Imlach. Harold Ballard would call him "a cancer on the team." He was traded to Philadelphia in 1982 and finished his career in Detroit. He scored 484 career goals and was inducted into the Hockey Hall of Fame in 1989. Dave Reece never played another NHL game after his February 7, 1976, nightmare at Maple Leaf Gardens.

Lop Off His Head, Roared Ballard

WHEN the Leaf team photograph was taken early in the 1977–78 season, backup goaltender (to Mike Palmateer) Gord McRae, wearing a short, neatly-trimmed black beard, posed with his mates. But when the annual Christmas cards were printed, with the team photo on it, McRae's beard was missing. The mystery of the missing beard was solved when Gardens' publicist Stan Obodiac confessed he'd not only eliminated the beard but he'd lopped off McRae's head as well — figuratively speaking. On Harold Ballard's orders, of course.

Obodiac had the photographer airbrush away McRae's 1977 head and replace it with a clean-shaven countenance from a 1976 photo.

"Now that Ballard's learned how to swap heads of players in photographs," mused Frank Orr of the *Toronto Star*, "how long will it be before he tries to swap heads among his real live players in an effort to help his team?"

Rocky's Debut

Late in the 1978–79 season the Leafs flew in high-scoring Rocky Saganiuk from the minors, where he'd scored 47 goals. Would this raw rookie, we wondered, become another big shooter, like Darryl Sittler or Lanny McDonald?

We had a rookie producer on our telecast that Saturday night — Brian Wayne, son of the late TV comedian Johnny Wayne.

Brian came up with a startling concept for the opening moments of our show. Dave Hodge and I were in a small room next to the TV studio when he confided in us.

"Here's what's going to happen," he announced. "We'll have Rocky Saganiuk dress up in a Maple Leaf sweat suit and we'll have a camera follow him down Church Street as he jogs towards the Gardens.

"The theme song from the *Rocky* movie (with Sylvester Stallone) will be blaring in the background. Saganiuk will jog through the corridors and into the Leaf dressing room, our cameraman right behind him. As he runs along he'll raise his arms in the air like Rocky Balboa did in the movie. What a way to open our telecast! It'll be sensational! We're going to tape it in about an hour."

He sat down and about ten minutes later Leaf general manager Jim Gregory stormed into the room.

"Who the bleep's been talking to Saganiuk?" he growled. "And what's all this crap about having my rookie running down the street in a sweat suit before the biggest game he's ever played? That's the stupidest idea I've ever heard of. Who dreamed this one up?"

Hodge and I remained silent while Brian Wayne tried to explain. But Gregory jumped in again.

"Listen, you little bleep. You should know better. I bring a rookie up and you try to make an actor out of him before he gets his skates on. The kid's over in our dressing room and he's so uptight about facing the bleepin' cameras he can hardly spit. No way he's going to be part of your bleepin' opening. And next time, fellow, check with me before you come up with any hare-brained schemes like this one."

He stalked out of the room. Hodge and I looked at each other and tried to suppress our laughter while Brian Wayne sat there stunned.

Welcome to *Hockey Night in Canada*, kid. Looks like Saganiuk isn't the only rookie who's facing an uncertain future.

The Missing Gondola

ALL writers and broadcasters live for the day they can claim a scoop, an exclusive story that is theirs alone. One August day in 1979, writer Rick Boulton stumbled on a story that shook the hockey world — and cost him his job. Here's how Rick recalls it:

> I was the editor of the Leaf program in the late '70s and I'd been doing that job for about six years. Even though I wasn't a staff employee at the Gardens, I had the run of the place. For the longest time, Harold Ballard couldn't figure out who the hell I was. He asked me once, "Who are you, anyway?" and I replied, "Well, I'm with the program, Mr. Ballard." He said, "Oh, glad to meet you. You're with the CBC." He thought I was with a TV program. So I explained that I edited the program sold at the Leaf games.

Because I got in free to every event, I used to attend some of the rock shows and concerts. I'd bring dates to see these performances and we'd slip up to the press box. One summer night in 1979, during a Bee Gees concert, I happened to look across the arena and I noticed something was missing. There was a gap where Foster Hewitt's gondola should have been. But it was gone!

So the next day I played detective and asked around. Jesse James, the assistant building superintendent, told me that the gondola had been broken up and sent to the Gardens' incinerator.

What a shock it was to hear that.

Because I was editing the hockey program eight months of the year, I had little to do in the summer months. So I freelanced. And this was a whale of a story. The best part was, nobody else had it.

I hotfooted it down to the *Toronto Star* and they said, "Geez, that's a great story. We want it. Get on the phone and call everybody. Get Frank Selke Sr., chairman of the Hockey Hall of Fame. Talk to Lefty Reid, curator of the Hall of Fame. Call Foster! Get a bunch of people to comment on this great loss." So I did. I had from five o'clock to nine o'clock to do this. Nine p.m. was the deadline. I talked to a dozen people and threw the story together. But now it was time to get Ballard to talk. I desperately needed a comment from him.

When I called him that night the woman who answered the phone said Harold was busy and didn't want to talk to anybody. So I decided to tell a little fib. I said, "Tell him it's vital I talk with him. Tell him . . . tell him Foster Hewitt has just died."

Well, that got the old boy's attention. Ballard scooted to the phone and he gave me some wonderful quotes about Foster and his many contributions to the game. Once he finished, I said innocently, "By the way, Mr. Ballard, what have you done with Foster's gondola?" He told me he had it thrown in the incinerator. I said, "Why?" and he said, "Because it was no bloody good to anybody." He followed up with some colourful quotes and now I had the complete story.

The next day the *Toronto Star* emblazoned the story in red ink all over the front page. The headline read: "Oh, No! Pal Hal Has Trashed Foster's Gondola!"

I had quotes from men like Frank Selke Sr. and Clarence Campbell, who expressed their shock and outrage. Mr. Campbell said, "Our troops in World War Two listened to games described by Foster from that famous gondola. How could he have thrown it in the incinerator?"

The next day, still gloating over my coup, I got a call from Stan Obodiac. He said, "Rick, you're out! Ballard says that was the dirtiest, sneakiest trick ever played on him. You told him Foster Hewitt had croaked and he's livid. He says you'll never be allowed in the Gardens again."

So that was it. I was banned from the building for the next ten years.

But there's a postscript to my story. My employers, the men who produced the programs for Leaf games, still wanted me to keep on writing for them. So I suggested I use the pseudonym Dick Oliver, because Oliver is my middle name, and continue to deliver stories for the program. Suddenly stories started popping up by Dick Oliver. Obodiac, I was told, went up and down the press row on hockey nights, trying to identify Dick Oliver, for he prided himself in knowing everybody. Finally somebody told him they thought Oliver was the sports editor of the Stratford *Beacon Herald*.

A few days later, Earl McRae, another writer who was often in Ballard's bad books, made an infrequent appearance in the press box and brought a friend along. Tried to sneak him in. Obodiac hustled over to greet the pair and said to McRae, "Hi Earl, who's your friend?" McRae grinned and invented a position in the media for his pal. "Stan, say hello to the sports editor of the Stratford *Beacon Herald*." Obodiac threw out his hand and said, "Glad to meet you, Mr. Oliver. I want you to know I read your stuff all the time."

McKenny's Memories

J IM McKenny was a colourful and often comical defenceman who played for the Leafs from 1965–66 to 1977–78. Since retiring from the game he has become a popular sportscaster with CITY-TV in Toronto.

One thing a *Hockey Night in Canada* commentator could always count on from McKenny was a good quote and a funny story. I asked him once about his views on violence in hockey. He said,

I always felt the violence made me play better. I never skated so fast in my life as I did when the game got violent — just staying away from it.

One night we were playing against John Ferguson and the Montreal Canadiens. What a tough bird that Fergie was! I'm standing at the blue line and Fergie is carrying the puck down the ice. Just then Billy MacMillan, one of our forwards, cuts him off, gets a shoulder into him and knocks him flat. Geez, did he land hard. Billy must have been crazy to do it. When Fergie staggers to his feet, his nostrils flaring, the first Leaf he sees is me. I knew right away he thought I'd bowled him over. So for two periods he's chasing me all over the ice trying to kill me and MacMillan is loving it. Finally I had to scream at Fergie over my shoulder, "For God's sake, Fergie, get off my case. It wasn't me who hit you, it was MacMillan. Go chase him!" On the next shift he grabbed MacMillan and beat the crap out of him. Thank God it wasn't me.

During the 1973–74 season, the Leafs made a good deal, getting Timmy Ecclestone from Detroit in exchange for Pierre Jarry. I loved Tim because of his sense of humour. We were playing in Philadelphia one night and Tim and I were sitting on the bench, not playing too much. Now Flyer tough guy Dave Schultz — he's been in a million fights — goes skating by our bench and Timmy yells at him, "Hey, Schultz, you asshole, you're going to get yours tonight." That broke me up and I started laughing. Then Schultz stops and shouts back, "I'll break your face, you little faggot!"

I turned and said, "Tim, did you hear what he said to you?" But Tim wasn't there. He was crouched over, hidden from Schultz's glare, pretending he was lacing up his skates. So Schultz assumed it was me who'd challenged him. I paid for that one, with Schultz whacking away at me every chance he got. Of course Timmy thought it was hilarious.

One more Tim Ecclestone story, okay? We were playing at the Montreal Forum one night and the Habs hadn't lost at home for something like 38 games. That may have been the night a guy came in our dressing room before the game and said, "Gee, it's quiet in here." I told him, "You'd be quiet too if you knew you were going to get the shit beat out of you in the next couple of hours." Anyway, we were playing brutal hockey. Our coach, John McLellan, a real good guy, gave us a pep talk before the game. He said, "Come on, guys, my ass is on the line. Looks like I'm going to be fired pretty soon, so give it your best shot out there tonight."

Our best wasn't very good because we come back in the room trailing 2–0. But we'd been outshot like 21–1 and McLellan is fuming. He says, "One shot, one goddam shot! You guys make millions to play hockey and all you can manage is one shot. I can't believe it!" And he began to tear the room apart, kicking waste baskets and throwing towels around. Then he went outside to cool off, slamming the door behind him.

That's when Tim stood up and faced his teammates. "Okay," he said, "Who's the wise guy?"

7

THE EIGHTIES AND NINETIES

Surely There Are
Better Days Ahead

ORONTO'S Stanley Cup hopes had soared in the spring of 1978. In the playoffs a quick trouncing of the Los Angeles Kings and a stirring upset victory over the Islanders in round two, with Lanny McDonald's breakaway goal in overtime of game seven clinching the series, had propelled the Leafs into the semifinals versus Montreal. Even though the weary Leafs fell to the Habs in four straight games, it was the first time in 10 years a Toronto team had advanced so far, and there was promise of much bigger things to come.

But it was not to be. Within four seasons only one player from the group that silenced the Islanders would still be around. The trades began with then general manager Jim Gregory and ended with Punch Imlach, back for a second term. Gregory shipped defenceman Randy Carlyle and centre George Ferguson to Pittsburgh. Hard-hitting Brian Glennie was dealt to Los Angeles, Jack Valiquette was sent to Colorado for a draft choice, and Trevor Johansen and Don Ashby soon followed him to the Rockies. Punch Imlach replaced Gregory and made more changes, some of them startling. Pat Boutette, a tough winger, was sent to Hartford for Bob Stephenson, who fizzled. In a stunning move, Lanny McDonald was shipped to Colorado, along with Joel Quenneville, in return for Wilf Paiement and Pat Hickey. The Leaf players were so distraught at news of McDonald's departure that some wept openly. When their mood changed to anger, they ripped the Leaf dressing room apart. A day later, still angry, they shaved the genitals of rookie Rocky Saganiuk, who had dared to say, "Don't worry, guys, I'll take McDonald's spot."

McDonald later confessed he wanted to whack Imlach in the mouth when the Leaf manager stuck out his hand and wished him luck in Colorado.

Later, Imlach sent Tiger Williams and Jerry Butler to Vancouver. It was his one smart move because it brought Rick Vaive and Bill Derlago to the Leafs. In the off-season Imlach unloaded unhappy goaltender Mike Palmateer, a fan favourite, to Washington. He bought out the contract of right winger Ron Ellis, shipped Ian Turnbull to Los Angeles, and dealt Darryl Sittler, a future Hall-of-Famer, to Philadelphia for Rich Costello and a second-round draft choice.

From the team that showed such promise in 1978, only one player remained: Borje Salming.

Coach-Bashing Becomes Popular

P ERHAPS it began with the famous dart-throwing episode in a pub close to Maple Leaf Gardens. It was 1980 and several Leaf players, fed up with Punch Imlach's decisions, used a newspaper with Imlach's photo in it as a dartboard. One of the dart-tossers, Dave Hutchinson, was gone before the day was over, traded to Chicago.

Leaf coaches in the '80s encountered a new breed of player. They were brash and outspoken and not easily intimidated. When Joe Crozier coached the club briefly in 1980, he pleaded with the players one night to turn in a top performance, otherwise he might lose his job. There was silence following his exhortation — until Ian Turnbull leaned to one side and unleashed a loud fart.

John Brophy was hired in 1986. He came with a reputation for being one of the meanest, toughest players ever to lace on skates. For years he'd terrorized opposing players in the old Eastern League. Brophy and his defence partner, Don Perry (one of the best fistfighters hockey has ever seen), were playing for the Long Island Ducks one night against New Haven. On the first shift they started an ugly brawl that sent the visiting players scurrying to their dressing room. And they refused to come back, despite the offer of $100 per player to return. "No way," they said. "Not with those two goons out there."

The game had to be cancelled.

One Leaf player who dared to dump on Brophy was Miroslav Frycer. At the end of the 1987–88 season, Frycer told reporters, "There's no way I'll ever play for that man again. Ninety percent of the players hate playing for him. But they're not going to say it. He's the first guy to panic behind the bench when we need a guy to calm us down. He's created a nightmare for this team, this city, for me and my family. I'll never be back." One Leaf, who requested anonymity, agreed with Frycer. He said, "Brophy ripped the heart out of every guy on this team, one by one."

Frycer was promptly traded to Detroit.

Leaf owner Harold Ballard, who refused to heed general manager Gerry McNamara's plea to fire Brophy the previous season, said of his coach, "Brophy's the best coach in the NHL and he'll be back behind the Leaf bench again next season."

And he was.

The Woeful '80s
and New-Look '90s

I N 1980–81, the Leafs set a standard for ineptness that would stick with them throughout the '80s. They finished last in their division (Adams) and ended up with 28 wins, 37 losses, and 15 ties for 71 points. They were worse the following season, when they moved to the Norris Division, ending the 1981–82 campaign with stats of 20-44-16 for 56 points. They moved up to third place in the Norris in 1982–83 with a 28-40-12 mark, good for 68 points, but slipped back to last place in 1983–84 with a dismal 26-45-9 showing for a total of 61 points. They plummeted even deeper into the division basement in 1984–85 with a measly 48 points (20-52-8) and improved by nine points the following season (25-48-7). In 1986–87, the Leafs tied Minnesota for last place in the Norris even though Toronto won seven more games than the previous year. They finished 32-42-6 for 70 points. Alas, they fell back again in 1987–88, winding up with a 21-49-10 mark and 52 points. They were a last-place finisher (again) in the Norris in 1988–89 with 62 points as a result of a 28-46-6 campaign. As the decade of futility ended, in 1989–90 they showed some promise with a third-place finish in their division, establishing a mark of 38-38-4 for 80 points. It was their first .500 season in 11 years.

In a decade when they were generally managed by Punch Imlach, Gerry MacNamara, Gord Stellick, and Floyd Smith, and coached by Imlach, Joe Crozier, Mike Nykoluk, Dan Maloney, John Brophy, George Armstrong, Doug Carpenter, and Tom Watt, they mustered only 266 wins, as opposed to 441 losses, and they gave up 637 more goals than they scored. No wonder, when Cliff Fletcher arrived on the scene, he had nowhere to take his team but up.

Cruel Maple Leaf Joke:
Highway 11, Maple Leafs 0

WHEN the Leafs won only 20 games under coach Dan Maloney in 1984–85, the late Gary Lautens, writing in the *Toronto Star*, asked readers to send him cruel Maple Leaf jokes. First prize (two tickets to a Leaf game) went to Michael Hall of Ajax for the following:

> Leaf goalie Ken Wregget was so depressed after blowing a 6–2 lead he jumped in front of the Toronto team bus — but it went right through his legs.

Second prize (FOUR tickets to a Leaf game) went to Olga Roberts of Toronto:

> Why are the Leafs like the Post Office?
> Because they both wear uniforms and don't deliver.

Other Lautens selections:

> What do you get when you cross a Leaf with a groundhog?
> Six more weeks of lousy hockey.

> Definition of a loser: A pregnant prostitute driving her Edsel to a Leaf game.

> Did you hear the Leafs have a new Chinese coach?
> Win Wun Soon.

> What do the Leafs and Warren Beatty have in common?
> Nothing. Warren knows how to score.

What do the Leafs and the Blue Jays have in common?
    Neither can play hockey.

I don't want to enter the Cruel Maple Leaf Joke contest because I'm afraid I might win the tickets.

What has 40 legs, is mean, and lives in the cellar?
    The Leafs — I lied about the mean part.

The man said, "My dog watches all the Leaf games on TV. Every time they lose he lies down and cries his eyes out." His pal says, "That's incredible. What does he do when they win?" The man said, "I don't know. I've only had the dog a couple of years."

Remember, this contest was held a few years ago, when the Leafs really were incompetent.

Vaive Gets Fifty

LEAF captain Rick Vaive was in the spotlight on March 24, 1982, at Maple Leaf Gardens. No Leaf in history had ever scored 50 goals in a season and Vaive was on the brink. He sent the crowd into a frenzy when he whipped a shot past goalie Mike Liut of the St. Louis Blues for the historic marker. He went on to score 54 goals that season, a Toronto team record. Three times in his career Vaive topped 50 goals. Gary Leeman, in 1989–90, became the second Leaf to top the barrier with 51.

In 1992–93, Dave Andreychuk scored 29 goals for Buffalo and (following a trade) another 25 goals for the Leafs, for a 54-goal season. In 1993–94 he scored 53 goals as a Leaf — one shy of Vaive's club record.

From "Chicken Swede" to "Super Swede"

AMONG the many glittering Leaf heroes, Borje Salming rates special mention because he anchored the Toronto defence for most of two decades and excelled in more than 1,000 games with his adopted team. Someday, surely, his craggy features will grace a plaque at the Hockey Hall of Fame. To Salming goes most of the credit for triggering the invasion of European players to the NHL in the '70s.

It all began when Leaf scout Gerry McNamara journeyed to Sweden in December 1972, to look at a goaltender. He saw Salming display great bursts of speed and outstanding blue-line skills and decided to recommend him to his employers. He praised him so highly that the reaction in the Leaf front office was a skeptical "This guy better be good." McNamara needn't have worried. Salming was more than good.

At that time a Swedish player could be acquired by paying $50,000 to the Swedish Ice Hockey Federation — a bargain in Salming's case. The Leafs also signed Inge Hammerstrom, a talented winger who averaged over 20 goals a season in his first years as a Leaf. But Leaf owner Harold Ballard sneered at Hammerstrom's clean play. When he said disparagingly, "That kid could go in the corners with six eggs in his pocket and not break one of them," it was the beginning of the end for Hammerstrom in Toronto. He was traded to St. Louis during the 1977–78 season, played one more season, and then returned to Sweden.

The Leafs also placed Anders Hedberg's name on their negotiation list and Hedberg would have been an outstanding addition to the roster. But Hedberg wanted to play on the same team as his friend Ulf Nilsson, who was on Buffalo's list. They decided that the only way they could play together in North America was to sign with the Winnipeg Jets of the WHA. In Winnipeg they juggled the puck like magicians, performing on a line with Bobby Hull. Winnipeggers vow it was one of the greatest lines in hockey history, and Manitobans know their hockey.

As for Salming, Ballard loved him like a son and rewarded him accordingly. By 1980 he was the highest-paid player in Maple Leaf history, pocketing a five-year contract worth $275,000 per annum, an option for six more years, and bonuses of all kinds that made "B-J" a very wealthy man. No wonder Salming said of Ballard, "Most people think he is crazy but I think he is a very nice guy."

It's interesting that Ballard signed Salming, not Imlach, who was the Leafs' general manager. Imlach travelled all the way to Sweden to discuss a deal with Salming and the negotiations went nowhere. Salming had a brief chat with Ballard and the deal was signed.

Salming quickly dispelled the notion that all Swedish players were "chickenshit." When he refused to back down from Philadelphia's "Broad Street Bullies" in the mid-'70s, leading rushes right into the thick of their flying sticks, elbows, and punches, Salming earned the respect of players throughout the league.

He had his problems as a Leaf. He was suspended for a few games when he admitted to experimenting with cocaine. He nearly lost the sight in his right eye during a playoff series with the Islanders in 1978. The blow from Lorne Henning's stick caused severe hemorrhaging and he lay in hospital for five days, his head wrapped in bandages. Then, the good news: he'd be able to return to hockey, his vision restored.

He was not an easy man to interview. In fact, he avoided the radio and TV reporters as much as possible. And he stayed in the background, saying little, all through the bitter war that broke out between Punch Imlach and the rest of the Leafs.

He never played on a Stanley Cup team but he was named to six All-Star teams. He starred on many Leaf teams that were often described as "dreadful."

Darryl Sittler once said, "There are very few athletes in any sport that have his quality, the ability to lift people out of their seats with a single move. We used to watch him and wonder what it was that made him so good. He'd play 30, 40 minutes a game with everybody taking shots at him. And he just kept bouncing back. He had great stamina, great courage."

Nykoluk and Maloney Bounce Reporter

IN January 1984, *Globe and Mail* sportswriter Al Strachan rapped Leaf coach Mike Nykoluk on the knuckles in print. Strachan had noticed that Nykoluk was having difficulty matching lines with his NHL rivals — even when the Leafs, playing at home, had the advantage of the last line change.

When Strachan strolled into the Leafs' dressing room after the next game, Nykoluk blew a fuse. He called Strachan every expletive he could think of and forcibly removed him from the room. "Get out of here, you bleeping bleep. You run me down, you son of a bleep. You're no bleepin' writer."

A *Globe* photographer captured the drama with his camera, and this infuriated assistant coach Dan Maloney. "You get some good shots?" he asked. "Good. Now get out of here, creep. If I ever see you in here again I'll bust that camera right over your head."

Harold Ballard supported his coaches and banned *Globe and Mail* reporters from the Toronto press box for the next two months. In March they were allowed back in "on probation." As one wag put it, "Now they can document firsthand the team's inability to make the playoffs."

Tiger Tales

SEVERAL years ago Tiger Williams wrote a delightful book about his life in hockey. A major portion of the book, *Tiger: A Hockey Story*, dealt with his years as a Leaf. Some of his comments and revelations about the team's most turbulent era are worth repeating.

On Harold Ballard: When he was a rookie, the Leaf trainer told Williams that Ballard respected people who stood up to him. Conversely, he liked to intimidate players who feared him. When Ballard turned on Williams one day and called him "a goddam little stubble-jumper from Saskatchewan," Williams shot back, "That's better than being a fat old bastard from Ontario."

On Dave Keon: While most fans adored Dave Keon as Leaf captain, Williams claimed Keon never did what a captain should do. Instead of taking Williams aside in his rookie season and offering encouragement, Keon wore him down with criticism. When Williams had heard enough of Keon's nagging, he grabbed him by the tie in an elevator one day and said, "Listen, Davey, I don't need this shit. Now get off my back or I'll break your neck."

On defenceman Jim McKenny: While Williams was furious over the amount of drinking his mates indulged in, it didn't prevent him from liking them. Jim McKenny, despite a serious drinking problem, was funny and kind. Williams cites the time McKenny was driving the wrong way down a one-way street when he was pulled over by the police. When a cop pulled open the car door, McKenny fell out at his feet. "Have you been drinking?" asked the cop. "No officer, I always look like this," replied McKenny.

On Ian Turnbull:

Turnbull was quick and smart but he was a pure rebel. The more he rebelled, the more Ballard liked him. He

didn't work at practice, he didn't look after his body. It disgusted me that so much talent was being thrown away and that a coach like Roger Neilson could be wrecked by a guy who couldn't look after himself. I had this urge to go out and clobber him, really give him a working over. Once, I joined Neilson in the sauna at Maple Leaf Gardens and said, "Roger, if you don't get rid of Turnbull he'll get rid of you." The bizarre thing was that Ballard loved Turnbull, the player who probably could do the most damage to his dream of having a winning team.

On the only time Williams cried after a game: In the spring of 1978 the Leafs upset the Islanders in a dramatic playoff series and lost to the powerful Canadiens in the Stanley Cup finals. A year later they lost to Montreal again, this time in a quarterfinal matchup. In the final game of this series, Williams took a costly high-sticking penalty in overtime. He recalls:

I paid the full price — and it cost us the game. Larry Robinson, the man I was supposed to have high sticked, scored the winning goal. On the penalty, there's no doubt my stick was up, but it wasn't over the boards and for me to high stick Robinson I would have needed a friggin' ladder. When I came out of the box when the game ended, I just went for Myers (the referee). I wanted to kill the son of a bitch. Robinson headed right for me and grabbed me; only a guy as big, strong and fast as Robinson could have done it. He wrapped his big arms around me and said, "Forget it, kid, it was a horseshit call but I'll take you fishing in the summer." The big guy saved my neck because if I'd got hold of Myers, I'm sure I would have done him serious damage. In the dressing room I cried. I'd never done that before — and I haven't done it since.

On Punch Imlach:

Right from the start, Imlach created a harsh, new atmosphere in the Gardens. It was as though we were stepping back in time. No one was allowed to go into Imlach's office without a tie. Once, I had to go see Ballard who had no dress code regulations. I wasn't wearing a tie. Imlach saw me leaving Ballard's office and he shouted, "Hey, Williams, what are you doing without a tie?" I said I wasn't aware I needed one to visit Ballard. Imlach fined me $150. It was a typical Imlach touch — petty, insulting. He treated us all like children.

On his last game as a Leaf:

We were in New York and I had a premonition that this would be my last night in a Maple Leaf uniform. After the game, we travelled to the Holiday Inn in Uniondale. We had a late dinner down the block and over the meal I told some of the guys, "If I'm still here at the end of the week, I'll pay for everyone's meal." When I returned to the hotel, Dick Duff, who by then was Imlach's puppet, came up to me and handed me an envelope. He said, "You got traded." Inside the envelope was an air ticket back to Toronto. I asked Duff where I'd been traded. He said, "I can't say."

On his last conversation with Imlach:

I went into the bar and found Imlach sitting at a table in a dark corner. He said I was traded to Vancouver but I couldn't tell anybody at this point. I told Imlach I had done everything I could for the Maple Leafs and for him as a boss. That was because I was a professional and because I felt a debt to Ballard and Clancy. I had gone through life trying not to let people down but Imlach was something else. I told him the Lanny McDonald trade was garbage and that Sittler was one of the best leaders the game had to offer. I said that maybe Punch Imlach was once a great hockey man but it was gone now. I leaned across the table and said, "Punch, you've lost it boy." He went crazy when I said those things. He said that he was the last guy to bring the Stanley Cup to Toronto and he was the only man in the world who could bring it back. He said that the club and the players were nothing without him, and I'd better tell the guys before I left that it was going to be his way or the highway. I said that he should take a real good look at the situation and get rid of all the bullshit or else make way for someone who would.

On Jerry Butler (traded to Vancouver with Williams in return for Rick Vaive and Bill Derlago):

Imlach left the hotel before he could talk to Butler so it took me quite a time to convince Jerry that he was part of the deal. Butler asked the coach, Floyd Smith, and he said he didn't know what was going on. We flew back to Toronto where we were booked first class to Vancouver. On the way to the airport, Jerry said to me, "For your sake, Tiger, it better be true that I'm traded." He was a good guy, Butsy. He played his guts out for the Leafs and nobody even bothered to say goodbye.

Pal Hal's
Most Outrageous Acts

ON April 11, 1990, Harold Ballard, the irascible owner of the Toronto Maple Leafs since 1972, died peacefully in his sleep. His body succumbed to diabetes, kidney failure, and a weak heart. He was 86. He fought with his players, his family, sportswriters and broadcasters, the Soviets, and anyone else who looked like they wanted to scrap. His Toronto teams were often woefully weak, and finished .500 or better in only six of the 18 seasons he was in charge. They never finished higher than third in any division of the NHL. If someone were to prepare a top-ten list of Ballard's most bizarre behaviour, it might look like this:

1. ❑ IN 1928, Ballard appears at the Winter Olympics in Switzerland as the assistant hockey coach. A noncompetitor, he talks his way into becoming the flag bearer in the Olympic parade, depriving a bona fide athlete of the honour. Later he steals an Olympic flag. Four years later, he takes his Sea Fleas team to the world hockey championships in Prague. His undisciplined players are involved in many brawls on the ice and off. Ballard is thrown in jail after a fracas in Paris. His Sea Fleas become the first Canadian team to lose a world title.

2. ❑ IN 1965, Ballard brings the Beatles to Maple Leaf Gardens. On a blistering hot summer day, he turns the heat up in the packed building, cuts off the water flow to the drinking fountains, and holds the show up for over an hour. Hundreds of parched fans pass out, while hundreds more line up for soft drinks that are sold in large containers only. Ballard books a second show for the same day and when the Beatles' manager

protests, Ballard says, "They'd better perform or the fans who've bought tickets will tear them apart."

3. ❑ IN 1972, Ballard is charged with and found guilty of 47 counts of fraud and theft totalling $205,000. He is sentenced to three concurrent three-year terms and serves several months in jail.

4. ❑ IN 1973, released from prison on a three-day pass, he tells reporters Millhaven Penitentiary is akin to a country club, with steak dinners and colour TVs available to all the inmates. His comments anger Canadians from coast to coast and are discussed in Parliament.

5. ❑ IN 1974, Ballard rents the Gardens to Johnny Bassett and the Toronto Toros of the WHA for $15,000 per game. But the arena is in semi-darkness for the Toros' home opener. "The TV lights will cost you extra," he tells an enraged Bassett. The additional cost is $3,500 per night. He also removes the cushions from the team benches. "Let 'em buy their own cushions," he mutters.

6. ❑ IN 1978, Ballard buys the Hamilton Tiger Cats football team for $1.5 million and during his stint as owner attendance drops 42 percent. He loses $20 million on the venture and sells the team 11 years later to the City of Hamilton for a dollar. He tells Dick Beddoes, "What can you say about those clucks running Hamilton (the city). One guy over there is growing marijuana (an alderman had been charged with growing the plants in his cellar) and all the others are smoking it."

7. ❑ IN 1985, Ballard quarrels with all three of his children and denounces them through the media. They object to his relationship with Yolanda MacMillan, a 49-year-old divorcee who served time in prison for conspiracy to commit fraud. Ballard cancels a hockey game scheduled at the Gardens when he discovers that his daughter's son is on one of the teams. "Sometimes I think I'm surrounded by lunatics," he says. "Them and her."

8. ❑ BALLARD fires his son Harold Jr. from his job at Davis Printing, a Gardens-owned subsidiary, after he learns that Harold Jr. told a CBC reporter, "My dad once stuck my finger in a light socket when I was young and then told my mother he was 'just giving the kid some juice.'"

9. ❑ IN 1979, Ballard orders Foster Hewitt's famous gondola taken down and incinerated to make room for more high-priced luxury boxes. Ballard then announces he's saved Foster Hewitt's chair from the gondola. He rounds up several old chairs and has them painted red, with Foster Hewitt's name spelled out on the back. He tells reporters he sold all the chairs at five bucks apiece. Author's note: In all the years I worked with Foster Hewitt in the gondola at Maple Leaf Gardens I never noticed that he had a special chair. Certainly he didn't have his name painted on any of them.

10. ❑ IN 1979, Ballard is interviewed on Barbara Frum's CBC radio show *As It Happens* and infers that women are best in one position — on their backs. He doesn't actually say as much but the inference is clear. He also says, "They shouldn't let women on the radio. They're a joke." A few days later, a group of women picket the Gardens. They shout "Down with sexist Harold." Women who call him personally to complain hear him ask, "What's the matter, baby? Can't you find yourself a man? You want my body?"

––––––––––

Harold Ballard was inducted into the Hockey Hall of Fame as a builder of hockey in 1977. Why?

Fletcher Gets Full Marks

T HE revival of Leaf fortunes in the '90s can be traced to, and depends on, one man — president and general manager Cliff Fletcher.

The late Donald Giffen, who acted as the chief decision-maker around Maple Leaf Gardens following the demise of Harold Ballard, made one brilliant decision on July 1, 1991: he hired Cliff Fletcher to breathe some life into the moribund Toronto franchise.

It was a decision that angered Steve Stavro, Giffen's chief rival and co-executor of the Ballard estate. Stavro believed that Fletcher's salary — $4.5 million over five years — was excessive. He also felt that giving Fletcher almost total control was not a wise management decision. It's surprising that Fletcher accepted the position, since he knew that Stavro was en route to the CEO's chair at the Gardens and the grocery-store magnate could dismiss him once Stavro occupied Ballard's old chair.

But Stavro, a self-made multimillionaire, is nobody's fool. He didn't get to be one of Canada's most successful and wealthiest entrepreneurs by dumping talented people. While still unhappy with the terms of Fletcher's contract, he opted to sit back and see what the veteran hockey man could do.

"I'll do everything I can to re-establish the pride and tradition of this great franchise," Fletcher promised.

During the next few months he stamped the name "Fletcher" on a number of transactions and convinced long-suffering Leaf fans he was the ideal man for the job. Prior to Fletcher's arrival, the Leafs had finished out of the playoffs in three of their last four seasons. Once he grabbed the throttle, they improved by 32 points in one season, established a club record for points with 99, and marched into the 1992–93 Stanley Cup semifinals. They were just as solid the following season.

In 1993 Fletcher was named the *Hockey News*'s 1992–93 NHL

Executive of the Year as well as the *Hockey News*'s Man of the Year. In just three years on the job in Toronto, Fletcher was able to obtain players like Mats Sundin, Grant Fuhr (later traded to Buffalo), Doug Gilmour, Jamie Macoun, Mike Gartner, Dave Andreychuk, and a tough new coach in Pat Burns. Fletcher's wheeling and dealing all but erased the memory of Toronto's sad-sack clubs of the '80s and generated optimism that a Stanley Cup may be in reach before the end of the century.

Next to the blockbuster trade with Calgary that put Doug Gilmour in a Leaf uniform, Fletcher's most interesting acquisition was Pat Burns. On May 29, 1992, the former policeman was introduced as the Leafs' 22nd head coach. After four seasons behind the Montreal Canadiens' bench, Burns joined Toronto as the winningest coach in the NHL from 1988 to 1992. Only Glen Sather of the Oilers could claim a better winning percentage since 1983–84.

In his rookie season as Leaf coach, Burns guided the club to a 44-29-11 record and followed up with a 43-29-12 mark in 1993–94. No Leaf team had ever compiled consecutive 40-win seasons. Under Burns in 1992–93, the Leafs established club records for most wins (44) and points (99), home-ice wins in one season (25), playoff wins in one season (11), and playoff games in one season (21). The club's improvement by 32 points from the previous season was the most dramatic in Toronto hockey history and Burns was looked on as somewhat of a miracle man. His efforts were recognized by the league's broadcasters, who named him winner of the Jack Adams Award (Coach of the Year) for 1992–93.

Killer Trade
Turns Leafs Around

THE key players in the 1992 trade that dramatically changed the face of the Toronto Maple Leafs and the Calgary Flames were Doug "Killer" Gilmour and Gary Leeman. They might easily have been swapped one for one. But no, new Toronto general manager Cliff Fletcher and Doug Risebrough, his Calgary counterpart, couldn't leave it at that. They kept talking and adding bodies and soon it became a five-for-five blockbuster exchange, the biggest trade in NHL history.

To review: On January 2, 1992, the Leafs sent underachieving winger and former 50-goal-scorer Gary Leeman, inconsistent defenceman Michel Petit, a prospective big-league blue-liner (Alexander Godynyuk), a hard-working enforcer (Craig Berube), and a backup goaltender (Jeff Reese) to the Flames in return for Doug Gilmour (one of the league's top centres), highly regarded defenceman Jamie Macoun, veteran defender Ric Nattress, backup goaltender Rick Wamsley, and left wing prospect Kent Manderville.

The largest previous swap in the NHL took place in 1950, a nine-player deal between the Detroit Red Wings and the Chicago Blackhawks.

Ironically the trade talks involving Gilmour and Leeman began a year earlier, when Cliff Fletcher was the Flames' general manager. When he joined the Leafs he worked out the deal with Risebrough, his protege in Calgary.

Gilmour had bolted from the Flames a couple of days before the trade. He was unhappy with an arbitrator's award of $750,000 a year on a new contract and was angry when Risebrough wouldn't upgrade the dollars to what comparable centres were earning.

The Leafs were huge winners in this deal. Gilmour reached

superstar status as a Leaf while Leeman failed to show any semblance of his 50-goal form with the Flames, or later with Montreal.

Gilmour captured the Selke Trophy as best defensive forward in 1992–93 and was runner-up to Mario Lemieux for the Hart Trophy. He established club records for most points (127) and most assists (95) in one season in 1992–93 and was named the 15th captain in team history on August 18, 1994. He enjoyed two spectacular playoff seasons in '93 and '94, setting a club record for points with 35 in 1993. While injuries, and possibly advancing age, caused his play to slip in 1994–95, no player acquired so late in his career has become so overwhelmingly popular as Gilmour.

There's no doubt. The Calgary Flames were fleeced by Fletcher, their former boss.

THE LEAFS THROUGH
THE YEARS

1927: THE TORONTO MAPLE LEAFS are formed on February 14, when Conn Smythe convinces a group of investors to purchase the struggling St. Patricks franchise of the NHL. The original Leafs wear green and white uniforms with a maple leaf crest sewn on the front of the jersey.

1928: THE TEAM COLOURS are changed to blue and white.

1929: THE LEAFS sign left winger Harvey Jackson and play him on a line with Charlie Conacher and Joe Primeau. It's the birth of the famous Kid Line. Ace Bailey of the Leafs captures the individual scoring title in the NHL with 32 points.

1930: CONN SMYTHE spends a fortune ($35,000 and two players) to obtain defenceman King Clancy, a nine-year veteran, from Ottawa.

1931: CONSTRUCTION BEGINS on Maple Leaf Gardens in June. In a miracle of engineering, the building is completed in six months. On November 12, the Leafs lose their home opener (2–1) to Chicago in the new arena.

1932: WHEN THE LEAFS BEGIN TO SLIDE, Smythe replaces coach Art Duncan with Dick Irvin. The Leafs leap to first place and capture the Stanley Cup, defeating Chicago in the semifinals and sweeping New York 3–0 in the finals.

1933: THE LEAFS and Boston meet in a playoff game on April 3. The game requires six overtime periods before diminutive Leaf winger Ken Doraty ends it with a goal at the 164:46 mark. On December 12, Ace Bailey is almost killed in a game at Boston. Flipped high in the air by an Eddie Shore check, Bailey suffers a fractured skull and hovers near death for several days. Two months later a benefit game, the forerunner to the annual All-Star Game, is held for Bailey at Maple Leaf Gardens.

1936: JOE PRIMEAU retires, breaking up the Kid Line. King Clancy retires. The Leafs sign Syl Apps after he returns from the Olympic Games in Berlin, where he competed in the pole-vault event for Canada. Goalie Turk Broda is purchased from Detroit. Bob Davidson and Gordie Drillon join Apps as outstanding rookies.

1937: SYL APPS becomes the first winner of the Calder Trophy. Later he is named Canada's most outstanding athlete, the first time a hockey player has been so honoured. The Blackhawks, using substitute goalie Alfie Moore (pulled from a tavern) in one playoff game, upset Toronto in the Stanley Cup finals.

1940: DICK IRVIN resigns as Leaf coach and is replaced by Hap Day.

1941: CONN SMYTHE, 47, leaves Toronto for wartime duties and Frank Selke takes command as team general manager.

1942: THE LEAFS lose the first three games of the Stanley Cup finals to Detroit. Hap Day makes player changes and the Leafs storm back to win four straight and the Stanley Cup.

1944: LEAF DEFENCEMAN BABE PRATT assists on six Toronto goals in a 12–3 rout of Boston, establishing an NHL record.

1945: THE LEAFS welcome back Conn Smythe, who was wounded during the war. Goalie Frank McCool shines in the playoffs, racking up three consecutive shutouts over Detroit in the finals. The Leafs win the Stanley Cup in five games.

1946: FOR THE FIRST TIME in 16 years, the Leafs miss the playoffs. Babe Pratt is sent to Boston. Newcomers include Gus Mortson, Jim Thomson, Bill Barilko, Howie Meeker, and Vic Lynn.

1947: THE LEAFS win the Stanley Cup on April 19. Ted Kennedy scores the winning goal in a 2–1 victory over Montreal in game six. The Leafs are the youngest Cup winners in history. In October Smythe trades Bob Goldham, Gus Bodnar, Ernie Dickens, Gaye Stewart, and Bud Poile to Chicago for star centre Max Bentley and journeyman Cy Thomas.

1948: THE LEAFS win their second straight Stanley Cup, ousting Detroit in four games in the finals.

1949: THE LEAFS win their third Cup in a row. In the semifinals, they eliminate Boston in five games. In the finals, they dispose of Detroit in four. For coach Hap Day it is a remarkable achievement: five Stanley Cups in eight seasons.

1950: AFTER DEFEATING DETROIT in 11 straight playoff games, the Leafs succumb to the Red Wings in the Stanley Cup semifinals. In the off-season, Joe Primeau replaces Hap Day as Leaf coach.

1951: THE LEAFS reach the Stanley Cup finals and play five overtime games with Montreal before a winner is declared. Toronto defenceman Bill Barilko is the hero, scoring at 5:51 of the first overtime. A few weeks later he dies in a plane crash.

1952: THE CBC and *Hockey Night in Canada* begin telecasting games from Maple Leaf Gardens.

1953: KING CLANCY replaces Joe Primeau as Leaf coach.

1954: CONN SMYTHE, 60, steps down as general manager of the Leafs but retains presidency. Hap Day replaces him as general manager.

1955: TED KENNEDY retires as Leaf captain and is replaced by Sid Smith.

1956: HOWIE MEEKER replaces King Clancy as Leaf coach.

1957: GEORGE ARMSTRONG begins an 11-year reign as captain of the Leafs. Hap Day resigns as general manager. Billy Reay is the new coach. Foster Hewitt turns the play-by-play broadcasting of the Leaf games over to his son Bill.

1958: THE LEAFS sign 33-year-old goalie Johnny Bower. The club hires Punch Imlach, a relatively unknown executive, as assistant general manager. Promoted to general manager in November, Imlach fires Reay and takes on the dual role of general manager–coach.

1959: CALLED "The Cinderella Team," the Leafs edge their way into the playoffs with a late-season surge. They oust Boston in the semis but lose to Montreal in the finals.

1960: TORONTO ACQUIRES Red Kelly from Detroit in return for Marc Reaume. The Leafs reach the finals but lose to Montreal in four straight games.

1961: CONN SMYTHE is succeeded as Leaf president by his son Stafford. Stafford Smythe, Harold Ballard, and John Bassett buy controlling interest in the Gardens and the Leafs for $2 million.

1962: THE LEAFS dethrone Chicago and capture the Stanley Cup for the first time in 11 seasons. Dick Duff scores the winning goal in the 2–1 Toronto victory in game six. The Leafs triumph, four games to two.

1963: THE LEAFS finish in first place for the first time in 15 years, with 82 points, one more than Chicago. The Leafs defeat Montreal in a five-game semifinal series and win a second straight Stanley Cup by ousting Detroit, also in five games.

1964: THE LEAFS trade Dick Duff, Bob Nevin, Arnie Brown, Rod Seiling, and Bill Collins to New York for Andy Bathgate and Don McKenney. The club wins a third straight Stanley Cup, with the two newcomers playing a big role. Bob Baun scores an overtime winning goal in game six while playing on a cracked ankle bone.

1965: JOHNNY BOWER and Terry Sawchuk win joint possession of the Vezina Trophy, an NHL "first." A new award, the Conn Smythe Trophy, is donated by Maple Leaf Gardens for the playoff MVP, and Jean Beliveau is the first winner.

1967: THE LEAFS celebrate Canada's centennial by defeating Chicago and Montreal in the playoffs to capture their 11th Stanley Cup. They become the oldest team (average age over 30) to win the trophy.

1968: PUNCH IMLACH trades Frank Mahovlich, Pete Stemkowski, Garry Unger, and the NHL rights to Carl Brewer to Detroit for Norm Ullman, Paul Henderson, and Floyd Smith.

1969: AFTER A PLAYOFF SERIES LOSS to Boston, Punch Imlach is fired. Jim Gregory replaces him as general manager. John McLellan is named coach.

1971: STAFFORD SMYTHE dies in hospital after a massive hemorrhage at the age of 50.

1972: HAROLD BALLARD, at the age of 68, as executor of Stafford Smythe's will, sells Smythe's shares in Maple Leaf Gardens to himself at market price and takes over control (71 percent) of the Maple Leaf organization. In October, Ballard is sentenced to three years in jail after standing trial on 47 fraud and theft charges involving an amount of $205,000. He serves 12 months.

1973: RED KELLY replaces John McLellan as Leaf coach. The team loses goalie Bernie Parent, centre Jim Harrison, and defencemen Rick Ley and Brad Selwood to WHA teams.

1976: CAPTAIN DARRYL SITTLER turns in an astonishing individual performance against the Boston Bruins, scoring six goals and adding four assists in an 11–4 rout. His record ten points are against Bruin goaltender Dave Reece. Sittler later scores five goals in a playoff game against Philadelphia. In September, Sittler scores the overtime winner for Team Canada against Czechoslovakia in the deciding game of the first Canada Cup tournament.

1977: A NUMBER OF NHL OWNERS, led by Harold Ballard, veto a merger proposal with the WHA. Six WHA franchises had agreed to join the NHL at a cost of $2.9 million each. Roger Neilson replaces Red Kelly as Leaf coach.

1978: THE LEAFS provide a major surprise, winning the seventh game of their quarterfinal series with the Islanders. Lanny McDonald's overtime goal ends one of the most dramatic series in Cup history.

1979: JOHN McLELLAN, assistant general manager, dies of a heart attack at the age of 51. Coach Roger Neilson is dismissed, rehired, dismissed again, and replaced by Floyd Smith. Harold Ballard hires Punch Imlach, his former general manager, who returns to the Leafs to replace general manager Jim Gregory. On December 28, Imlach trades Lanny McDonald and Joel Quenneville to Colorado for Wilf Paiement and Pat Hickey. To protest, Sittler resigns as team captain.

1980: FLOYD SMITH survives a car accident that leaves him with a broken left kneecap and other injuries. Smith is charged with impaired driving and criminal negligence causing death. Dick Duff becomes his temporary replacement behind the Leaf bench. Later, Joe Crozier is brought in to replace Duff.

Harold Ballard signs defenceman Borje Salming, 29, to an 11-year contract and convinces Darryl Sittler to restore the captain's C to his jersey. Conn Smythe dies at the age of 85.

1981: GERRY McNAMARA replaces Punch Imlach as general manager. Mike Nykoluk is named coach of the Leafs and John Brophy is hired as an assistant coach. Darryl Sittler is traded to Philadelphia for Rich Costello, a Providence College freshman, and a second-round draft pick. Sittler set Leaf records for goals (389), assists (527), and points (916).

1984: DAN MALONEY replaces Mike Nykoluk as Leaf coach.

1985: THE LEAFS set a new club record for most losses in a season — 52. At the entry draft, they select tough Wendel Clark as their number one choice. Frank Selke Sr. dies at age 92.

1986: RICK VAIVE is stripped of the team captaincy after he oversleeps. In June, Dan Maloney rejects a one-year contract offer and signs on to coach the Winnipeg Jets. John Brophy replaces Maloney as Toronto coach. King Clancy dies at the age of 83.

1988: HAROLD BALLARD fires Gerry McNamara and replaces him with the youthful Gord Stellick, 31. Ballard undergoes quintuple-bypass heart surgery on his 85th birthday. John Brophy is dismissed and replaced by 58-year-old George Armstrong.

1989: GORD STELLICK resigns and accepts an assistant manager's job with the Rangers. Floyd Smith replaces him. Doug Carpenter is hired to coach the Leafs.

1990: TOM WATT is hired to replace Doug Carpenter as coach. Harold Ballard dies. Steve Stavro is named as one of the three executors of his estate.

1991: CLIFF FLETCHER is appointed as CEO, president, and general manager on July 1.

1992: ON JANUARY 2, Doug Gilmour is obtained from Calgary, along with Jamie Macoun, Ric Nattress, Rick Wamsley, and Kent Manderville, in return for Gary Leeman, Michel Petit, Craig Berube, Alexander Godynyuk, and Jeff Reese. On May 22, Pat Burns is introduced as the 22nd coach in Leaf history.

1993: DOUG GILMOUR sets Leaf records with 95 assists, 127 points, and captures Selke Trophy as best defensive forward. Dave Andreychuk, acquired from Buffalo, becomes the first NHL player to record 50 or more goals with two different teams in one season (29 with Buffalo, 25 with Toronto).

1994: THE LEAFS trade Wendel Clark, along with Sylvain Lefebvre, Landon Wilson, and a first-round draft choice to Quebec, in return for Mats Sundin, Garth Butcher, Todd Warriner, and a first-round draft choice.